My Pretty... AND ITS UGLY TRUTH

My Pretty...AND ITS UGLY TRUTH

De'Vonna Bentley-Pittman

Foreword by Menia Buckner

For Mama, my rock

Un-forgiveness leaves the victim stuck in the prison of what was. Which do you want; freedom to live life, or slavery to your hurts?

~TD Jakes

FOREWORD

Secrets. Everybody has them. We can choose to disclose them to intimate friends or we can bury them deeply in our graves of shame; in the innermost alcoves of our consciousness, not recognizing that they have rooted themselves so far into our essence that, if unchecked, become the insidious driving force that shapes every life decision.

In *My Pretty and Its Ugly Truth,* De'Vonna Bentley-Pittman reveals her very personal and raw experiences of being plagued by incest, sexual abuse, controlling relationships and the effect it had on her life. Her coming-of-age journey from a misused "product of the streets" to an empowered advocate for those who feel powerless due to years of abuse is a fascinating one. Like so many others, she grew up in a single-parent household with a mother who worked hard to provide for her children.

The streets called her away from home, leading her into a tangled web of promiscuity – unhealthy relationships, drugs, pregnancy, and almost selling her very soul. In spite of everything she lost, she never lost the one thing that would propel her forward --- hope.

As a speaker, teacher, writer, and editor, who constantly looks for ways to inspire others, I find *"My Pretty…and Its Ugly Truth"* to be that kind of inspiration. I laughed, I cried, I winced, I gasped, I sighed…and now I *salute* De'Vonna Bentley-Pittman. She is the voice today for victims of sexual abuse careening down a desperate and confused path. She is that Moses, that Harriet Tubman of our time that can and will lead others to a promised land of hope…and to their very own beautiful truth.

-Menia Buckner

Introduction

From my Heart to Yours

My Pretty...and Its Ugly Truth is a work of nonfiction. I have rendered these details truthfully as I recall them. Circumstances and events come from my keen recollection and memory. Names of individuals have been changed to respect their privacy. These are my *truths*.

I'd become a professional, walking across boardrooms, schmoozing with politicians, middle class and upper middle class. I was smiling on the outside, but dying on the inside. I was *just* a girl from the projects with secrets. Secrets I couldn't share with anyone. My fondest memory of singing *"Yes Jesus loves me"* in a kindergarten program wouldn't make the others go away. Yes, there were many other memories. Secrets that I had told no one. For far too many years, those secrets made unhealthy relationships and bad decisions a welcome comfort.

Eventually, *those things* were archived deeply in my subconscious and I had no intention of ever retrieving them. I was too busy with life; too busy to feel sorry for myself, and above all, too busy to be ashamed.

I was able to maintain the façade as I gained access to financial resources, education, and social networks. The continuous widening of my social networks made the guise easier to maintain. At least that's what I thought.

Beneath the façade, I carried around visions of the things that had happened. The secrets had become layered with years and decades of pain, and I was grieving with every breath I took.

I sat in a board meeting one afternoon thinking about my life as I mentally charted how I had come to this point. And while the Hennepin County Commissioners continued to vote on important actions, details of years past took over my thoughts and I began to journal. I had mastered my duties as the committee clerk but continued to struggle with how to overcome my past.

The foundation of my soul was beginning to crack and I knew that sealing the cracks and giving myself permission to move forward with my truths would have to begin with me.

I could no longer hide behind the pretty face. Something massive was taking place and a paradigm shift had over ridden all of my fears. I could no longer fight it -- my truths *had* to be told. Five years ago I embarked upon a quest to find others that had been through the same things I'd gone through. I was 34 years old and the secrets were eating away at my core, but I wasn't alone. There were other women just like me who were ready to come forward. Though the secrets were eating away at our core they made us who were. Many of us were able to deal with stress in ways that others weren't. We didn't break down when the odds were against us because we'd been through worse things. The secrets provided us with a force field that protected us from life's turmoil, and we smiled and proudly hit behind it. We had a sixth sense that others didn't have. We had arrived at the point of being able to conform and cope in the real world *despite* our shared tragedies. Coping, meant that we had been broken and "pieced" back together. In many cases, we could pinpoint an abuser -- even through a television screen. We could almost read a person's motives. These are the things that we'd learned to do as *sexual abuse survivors or sexual violence survivors*.

As I stood on the corner that day waiting for my bus, I knew I had to tell my husband about my past. God had put a will to survive deep down in my soul, and every time an incident ripped away pieces, I was reminded that I had to get up and keep moving. There was a job to be done and no one could do *my job* but me. I knew my entire story and only I could tell it. Even when I contemplated suicide, something deep inside me said, "NO, you have work to do." 'Who would need me? Who would miss me?'

I tried to convince myself that when I was gone my family and friends would all mourn and go back to the way things were, but those defeating thoughts were deafened by my desire to live. For many years I held my head high to hide the things that I'd been through and to *project* the sovereign allegiance of a survivor. I smiled when I wanted to cry, I laughed when I wanted to grieve. I am one of many.

Now, I stand to give a full account of what I endured. I share these intimate details of my life in an effort to open the eyes of children, mothers, fathers and families that are dealing with this epidemic. Writing this book has been laborious. It has been to date the hardest thing that I've ever *had* to do. Much of what I say is not pretty. In fact, it *is* the ugly truth.

First, I had to ask myself some serious questions. Would revealing my truth while lying prostrate before my peers be worth never being able to hide again? Was it worth dissecting and placing on the table sensitive details of my past and of the chambers of my heart? People would be upset. Was that what I wanted? If disclosing my truths meant saving one little boy or girl, it would most definitely be worth all the sacrifices I have made.

Men and women who have been abused hide their shame, but they are among us…everywhere we turn. They are our cousins, sisters, brothers, aunts, uncles, friends, nieces, and nephews. They can be found in boardrooms, as college presidents, movie stars or living in gated communities. They can also be found in the most undesirable places -- crack houses, jails, in rehabilitation centers, on street corners prostituting, or worse, in the cemetery, dead.

So I walk with my head held high, the façade has dissipated. As a salute to all of those who are still struggling, I'm holding the torch for you. I'm praying for you and I believe in your deliverance. It can come today. You can be on the journey to healing. I am a living, breathing testimony.

Chapter 1

The Fight for My Life

In the synagogue, there was a man possessed with an impure spirit. He cried out at the top of his voice, "Go away! What do you want with us, Jesus of Nazareth? Have you come to destroy us? I know who you are – the Holy One of God!" "Be quiet!" Jesus said sternly. "Come out of him!" Then the demon threw the man down before them all and came out without injuring him. All the people were amazed and said to each other, "What words these are! With authority and power he gives orders to impure spirits and they come out!" And the news about him spread throughout the surrounding area.

Luke 4:33-37

I'd told myself that life was a dream and I could shape each day the way I wanted it to start and end. That wasn't the case. The things that I'd been through wouldn't just disappear, healing had to take place. Before healing could take place I had to dig deep into my past and discover why I'd ended up here in the first place. I needed to figure out what I was running from and how long I had been running.

The memories came flooding back and I couldn't keep up with my thoughts...

I was being chased and my feet weren't moving fast enough. This person, this thing wanted me. There was urgency in its chase. The dark figure closed in on me. I could not see its face, because I was running for my life. I remembered what I'd been told by my track coach, "You lose ground when you look back, don't look back!" I ran for dear life! As fast as my legs would carry me, I ran! It wanted something that I had, but there was nothing in my hand. There was an eerie feeling that this had nothing to do with what I had, but who I was. It wanted my soul, and I was afraid that tonight I may lose it!

"Wake up! Get up now! The time is near! The world is coming to an end! Arise and awake from your slumber!" I had been awakened from a nightmare by a loud voice blasting from the radio on my night stand. What had seemed so real only minutes before had turned out to be a frightening dream, but the voice on the radio was *real*. It was powerful and distinct.

The voice of Elder Hutton, the powerful pastor of Holy Ghost Deliverance Center continued to bellow through the radio that, on a normal day, didn't work due to bad reception. Bits of aluminum foil had been pressed together on the tip of the antenna to force a signal to connect and provide reception from the local radio stations. Elder Hutton's voice was easily understood as it sounded through the contraption. He was known for his tongue-talking, Holy Ghost-believing, foot-stomping demeanor, and we'd heard that he could cast out demons. He was 6'2," brown-skinned, clean shaven, and often wore a black suit with the white collar, the kind priests wear. It never crossed my mind to consider whether Elder Hutton was "good looking" or not because he was too holy of a man to rate him by worldly standards. Before you saw him the *Holy Spirit* preceded his entrance. Whatever you needed from the Lord, you could get it through Elder Hutton and it was common knowledge.

Elder Hutton's powerful voice was still blaring through the radio when I felt *it*. I jumped out of bed screaming because something was there with me.

I hadn't heard anyone enter the room, but I felt a darkness appear over me as if my body had been taken into a spaceship. My screams had been muffled. There were invisible eyes watching me through the walls. I looked from side to side and didn't see anything, but I could feel its terror! My breathing intensified. 'How would I escape this room?' I was desperately thinking of a way to get out! I quickly jumped back on top of the bed and turned around several times, trying to identify a figure. I didn't see anything, but there was an intense feeling beneath my feet.

The volume increased on the radio, and Elder Hutton's voice was gripping, full of highs and lows. It was clear that there was a pull in the atmosphere, and both peace and chaos were being released into the room. A battle between good and evil was occurring as I stood there. I could *feel* it. My mind raced. My heart sped up and the increased level of fear was followed by my empty screams as the evil presence intensified. There was no other human being in the room to save me from this evil. Something had been smothering my voice and preventing me from screaming for help.

After what seemed like an eternity I opened my mouth and my voice escaped. "Bryce, Bryce, help me!!!!!!"

I backed into the wall of the tiny bedroom I shared with my sisters. I knew that someone or something would have to save me. I would not escape its clutches unscathed. Bryce slowly walked into the room looking in every direction, his eyes wide open. He stood in the door and watched as I cried uncontrollably, screaming at the top of my lungs.

"He's here, and he's trying to kill me! He wants to kill me! He wants my soul! He wants my soul!" My brother was in shock and his eyes were huge with fear. He stood in the door and tried to deny with words what I'd clearly seen in his face.

"Go back to sleep. There's no one here but us," Bryce said, looking at me in total horror. He was usually not afraid of anything. He was our protector and we looked to him to take care of us. He was not the kind of person to back down from a mortal being, but today his fear had come from the immortal. My brother was fifteen and thought he was tough, but on this day, his eyes bulged so wide they looked like saucers. Bryce looked around the room to make sure no one was there with me. Standing in the doorway, he quickly motioned for me to follow him.

epped backwards out of the room and his fast transformed into a sprint down the stairs. I ran behind him as fast as my legs would carry me and shivered standing next to him. He pulled a phone number out of his pant pocket and quickly dialed. Mama always gave strict instructions that we were only to call her during emergencies. The oldest sibling at home was given a phone number to reach mama whenever she was away from the house. Bryce waited several minutes and when my mother picked up he yelled into the receiver, "Ma, something is wrong with this girl, and she said the devil wants her soul!"

Bryce shoved the phone into my chest, "Mama wants to talk to you." Before I could speak a word to mama the heels of my feet, then my toes, lifted off the floor. I looked down as my body was elevated into mid air. I couldn't feel my body. I was not in control of what was happening. Every limb had stiffened as my toes pointed downward and my eyes followed. Within seconds I was thrown from one side of the room to the other.

Bryce, helpless and frozen in horror watched from across the room with his mouth wide open -- he had found safety in the kitchen corner. I fearfully searched for his eyes while he evaded my gaze. No words were spoken between us. The phone cord was wrapped around my body and I landed on the floor, terrified. I had been propelled into the air and spat out by an evil force. I screamed to my mother that the devil was in our house. She was hysterical and pleaded for me to explain what had just happened. I couldn't speak, fear had overtaken me.

"I'm on my way home now. It'll be okay, just calm down." Mama was crying and praying, but I could not calm down. There was nothing she could do to help me and she knew it. Mama *had* to get home. Her prayer had no affect on what was happening in our home this time.

I dropped the phone and ran to the couch where mama found me rocking back and forth, murmuring and staring into space. I had no thoughts. My mind was not my own. I wrapped my arms around myself seeking comfort from the traumatic experience that had occurred. Suddenly, I began to hear a song playing in my head, but couldn't remember where I'd heard it.

Mama rushed over and sat next to me and gently asked what had happened. She'd always said things like, "Don't worry, it's in the Lord's hands, God will work it out, He's working it out for your good." But I could hear the nervousness in her voice and I knew that this spiritual thing that I was fighting could not be won by mere words, not this time. Mama's voice was shaky and I knew the faith she'd always seemed to have was being tested. It wasn't like my mother to fear anything. When I heard the tension in her voice, I knew that even she could not help me. I murmured, "He wants my soul." Mama leaned into my body with both arms wrapped around me. Her lips were touching my ear and I could feel the warmth of her breath's whisper trail from my ear down my neck.

"Did something happen in church last night?" I was in a daze, and though I didn't speak, I began to reminisce about the night before - the music now amplified and the scene in clear focus, the events from the night before unfolded in my thoughts.

I'd been invited to church by my aunt and uncle, who were staunch Christians, they were "sanctified" and *sho' nuff saved*. I was excited to see my cousins, but I'd heard that most of the kids in Elder Hutton's church were sanctified and that they were *different* from the kids in my house or my neighborhood. At this church, the kids praised God like adults did and behaved different from any kids I knew. I was in for an eye-opening experience. When we arrived at the service I didn't say much, but I observed everything that was happening around me. The piano played an old familiar tune, "Jesus, He will fix it, after while." I filed in after my cousins and sat down. The girls were wearing long skirts that fell right at their ankles. They seemed to be pure, different, *better*. They walked with their heads held high. They spoke proper English and crossed their legs at their ankles when they were seated. Many of them had both a mom and a dad that lived with them.

I sat straight up in my seat and thought to myself, 'I could be *better* too.' As I sat in the pew listening to the message from Elder Hutton, it felt good being there. I was able to relate because he used language that even youth could understand. I understood why so many families depended on him Sunday after Sunday to pour life into their children. He was teaching them the way to good, clean living.

Elder Hutton knew how to reach the masses. Several times during the message, I thought he was talking to me. "God has a calling on your life. You are going to be the Moses of your city. *You* are going to be the person in your family that is going to open doors, but you have got to listen and pay close attention to what God is saying to you. You MUST give your life to the Lord. He's going to use you to change a nation. You have a mantle on your life. God is calling you to first love Him unconditionally and to trust him to heal and deliver you. Don't be afraid, *my child*, it is okay, He's already won the battle. You will be tempted, but you have already been set free. You have been called out to serve a true and living God," he preached. I *knew* he was talking to me.

The service was at a high point when Elder Hutton walked away and the choir began singing, "Don't wait till the battle's over, shout now! You know in the end you're going to win!" They sang with such power, their voices were one sound. It was angelic and I could tell that only by hours of practice could a choir sound like this. It was the first time that I'd heard a song and believed that I could be cleansed and renewed. I could be free! Elder Hutton had been praying over this choir many years before I'd arrived and it was evident in the power being released throughout the sanctuary. This choir was changing lives! I'd never heard anything like it in my entire life. I felt like a new person.

I slept well that night, and had made up my mind that I was going to live a holy life. God would be my savior. But at the same moment that I had decided to live for God, a host of demons had been assigned to disrupt and change my destiny.

"De'Vonna! Don't you hear me talking to you?" Mama was no longer whispering, she demanded an answer. I continued to stare into space.

She looked over at my grandmother who had silently entered the house, "We have to call Elder Hutton and find out what is going on."

My grandmother was speechless as she walked into the kitchen and picked the phone up from the floor. We sat quietly in the living room waiting to hear back from Elder Hutton's office. It wasn't long before my uncle called back to report that Elder Hutton had given the okay for my mother to bring me to his office at the church.

Mama wrapped a blanket around me and slowly walked me to the car. Her protective right arm was positioned firmly around my shoulder, as she held her left arm around my waist. Her hand fell right across my belly button as if she was determined to keep my soul safely protected inside my body. Other than her faith, she had nothing else. The gun that she kept at the house would not fight a spiritual battle. Her faith had been shaken, but she was determined to fight. My soul belonged to God and nothing or anyone would stake claim to it. I was in a daze and still didn't speak. My grandmother and Bryce quietly followed. It was normally considered disrespectful for a child to sit in the front seat and have an adult sit in the back. This didn't seem to matter today.

Mama opened the front passenger door and made sure I was safely inside before she proceeded to walk around to the driver's side.

No one spoke a word during the five-mile drive to Elder Hutton's church. We entered and the deacon led us to his office. Elder Hutton was a quiet man when he wasn't preaching, but when he spoke or preached, he talked about the saving power of God. I thought it was funny when he said "Aise God" instead of "Praise God." He was known for his ability to cast out demons. He wasn't a *wanna-be-preacher*. He was the real deal. People had talked about the power of Elder Hutton for as long as I could remember. Some even stayed away from him because it was believed that he could identify spirits, good or evil.

When Elder Hutton stepped into the room, demons trembled and he was sure that his mission in life was to proclaim salvation. He did that with a conviction that hasn't been witnessed since he passed away, or as the saints would say, "Went on home to glory."

Elder Hutton looked at me and proclaimed, "This child got a demon in her and I gotta pray it out." He was a prayer warrior and believed that some things *only* came out by prayer and fasting.

He had no doubt that he was the man for the job. There were several other people in the room, including my mother, my aunt and uncle, my grandmother, and one of the deacons of the church. Elder Hutton had given strict instructions that once he started casting out the demons everyone needed to start "pleading the blood of Jesus." As instructed, they each began to chant, "The blood of Jesus, the blood of Jesus, the blood of Jesus." He had looked directly at my mother and warned her that she should not try to stop the deliverance service no matter what. "The devil wants you to think that we are hurting her," he said. He began speaking in "tongues," a native language for "sanctified" people. If a saint faithfully submitted to the ways of the bible, had put away their sinning ways and strived to live a sin-free life, they were "gifted" with a language that the devil could not understand. This language was used when praying for sick ones, *sin-sick* souls or simply to praise God. It would reach the heavens.

As soon as the saints began speaking in tongues it was time for business. Elder Hutton wasted no time playing with the devil. *This was war.*

He pulled out a small glass bottle filled with blessed oil blessed by bishops and other men of God and was believed to contain special powers. He poured oil into the palm of his hands and rubbed them together. When the mature saints prayed demons out of people, the children were to exit the room because the adults didn't want the demons to *jump* into the children. Children were too pure to defend themselves against evil spirits and we hadn't learned to be "saved enough to spiritually ward off demons." Elder Hutton walked up to me as I stood next to mama. He strategically rubbed the oil onto my forehead with pressure and then made a cross with the oil using the tip of his index finger and began chanting, "The blood of Jesus, the blood of Jesus, the blood of Jesus."

The deacon and my uncle were standing behind me. I fell limp as my lifeless body slid to the floor. It was as if they knew it would happen eventually, they were prepared to catch me and position my body flat on the floor. One of the deacons threw a white sheet over my bottom half as Elder Hutton followed me down to the floor and instinctively began praying over me. He was on his knees as he leaned over my body with one hand raised in reverence to God.

He summoned help from the almighty savior and continued to anoint my head with the oil that remained on his hands.

"You comin' out today devil! By the blood of Jesus we cast you out right now! The blood of Jesus prevails against you devil!" At one point mama could not take it anymore; her baby appeared to be in agony. She jumped up and hysterically yelled, "Let her go Elder Hutton, she's okay!" my mother screamed helplessly, "Lord, help my baby!" But, my body was now host to something dark and evil and its words escaped my lips. Its voice was vile and wicked, unlike mine. "You don't know me -- I'm in control, WE are not going anywhere!" Mama was in shock, but Elder Hutton demanded that she get it together or leave the room. She calmed down and nervously watched as Elder Hutton continued to declare that the demons were coming out. The deacon handed mama tissues as she wept quietly in the corner trying to contain her emotions. "In the name of Jesus, you will come out today!" Elder Hutton declared.

I remember being on the floor and the saints surrounding me in a circle praying for the *devil* to "let me go." As I lay on the floor I had an out-of-body experience and I saw a shell of myself lying on the floor spitting at Elder Hutton and telling everyone in the room that they were going to die that day. Elder Hutton was not fazed by the transformation I'd made right before his eyes and he never backed down.

After a long and tedious battle the demons had been dethroned. Elder Hutton signaled to my mother, giving her permission to comfort me, and then he smiled and walked away. I reached for mama and she lifted my small frame up from the floor and wrapped her arms around me. She held me close to her chest as she cried and promised that our life would never be the same. She promised that she'd protect me and love me like never before. My eyes were tired and swollen from the battle I'd been fighting, but the clinging darkness was no longer present. I stood on my feet without the help of any of the adults in the room. My body felt light -- the spiritual fight was over and good had prevailed against evil. My body was tired, but my spirit had been renewed.

The shell that once lay on the floor had been filled with something that would carry me through the darkest days of my life. I'd been delivered. Elder Hutton was my Moses. Was it an exorcism? I didn't feel evil. I hadn't killed anyone and I hadn't committed any crimes.

My spirit was released from whatever was haunting me and I was now free to finally enjoy being a child. The feelings of sadness would now be a thing of the past. Elder Hutton asked me to come to the radio station broadcast the next day to testify about God's goodness. I was excited because I never imagined being featured on a radio station. He and all the adults in the room had told me how much God loved me and that there had to be something great in my future, otherwise, God would not have delivered me at such a young age.

Mama and my grandmother drove me to the radio station. Their exuberance was contagious as we all walked proudly into the radio station. During the live broadcast, I openly proclaimed that God had changed my life. He'd made me new, pure, and clean, and it was a great feeling, unlike anything I'd ever experienced before.

From that day forward I couldn't show weakness because God had healed me and I couldn't allow people to think that God's power didn't completely heal. I remembered the scripture that Elder Hutton said I must read. It was the last thing he said to me before we left the radio station.

"Daughter, the devil ain't playin' with you, do you hear me? You keep yourself guarded, God is real, and so is the devil," then he opened his bible and began to read.

When the unclean spirit is gone out of a man, he walketh through dry places, seeking rest, and findeth none. Then he saith, I will return into my house from whence I came out; and when he is come, he findeth it empty, swept, and garnished. Then goeth he, and taketh with himself seven other spirits more wicked than himself, and they enter in and dwell there: And the last state of that man is worse than the first. Even so shall it be also unto this wicked generation."

MATTHEW 12:43-45

I kept repeating the last part of the scripture, *"And the last state of that man is worse than the first, AND the last state of that man is worse than the first..."*

One thing was for sure; people had begun to judge me. They'd all heard about my *exorcism*. I was placed in two categories, depending on who was judging. I was either an angel or a devil, but I used the next year to my advantage, especially at home.   I'd begun to tell my little sisters that they had to do whatever I wanted because I was "God's child." It worked for a while, but when the lights went out at night I wondered why the devil wanted my soul. I was thirteen years old and it would be several years before I could figure it out.

Bryce had been removed from Elder Hutton's office, but witnessed the comings and goings of the deacon as he waited outside the office. He said it gives him chills to even think about what happened that day. He vividly remembers the details of the deacon walking out of Elder Hutton's office and tying up the bags that I vomited in as the demons were cast out; "You threw up three times and they carried it all away," he said. My sister had hidden under her bed that morning. She remembers it as one of the most frightening days of her life. For years, my family referred to it as "the time the devil was in you."

Those events were frightening, but they were nothing compared to the things that had happened to me years before or the things that were to come.

Chapter 2

Mudville

Mud-ville: A defamatory word - Dirt and or of the dirt; excrement; the lowest or worst of anything; related to a person or a place.

My grandparents, Big Daddy and Big Mama were married for over fifty years -- until death did them part. They migrated from Greenville, Mississippi to East Chicago Heights in the early 1960s and raised fourteen children in the ghetto, the housing projects. The projects were simply row houses located thirty miles south of Chicago.

Big Daddy was a janitor at the local community center for many years. He also drove junk trucks around neighboring cities picking up salvageable items that he either sold to the highest bidder or gave to families in need. My grandmother worked sporadically cleaning houses or in restaurant kitchens when the family needed extra money. Big Mama also operated a candy store out of her project unit, and on the weekends we helped her package candy and cookies in sandwich bags to sell to the neighborhood children. East Chicago Heights was later re-named "Ford Heights." For most of their lives, my grandparents lived in the housing projects.

Long before my grandparents arrived, the town had survived with dirt roads and later became a township. Prior to those developments, this unknown town was a stop on Harriet Tubman's Underground Railroad. Ford Heights had once been part of an integral junction allowing hundreds of slaves to taste freedom!

As East Chicago Heights began to flourish, the roads were paved. Then, a police station, a library, radio station, schools, and stores were built; this assured that the new town would be around for many years to come.

Ford Heights, now a town of dilapidating row houses that we called "projects," was once my home. The very mention of *Ford Heights* instantly delivered a picture of "projects and poor folk" to the minds of *outsiders*. And the neighboring city folk referred to Ford Heights as "Mudville." The projects were separated into four major subdivisions self-titled by its inhabitants. "The Bronx" was filled with young, single mothers and their children. There were a few older women, but for the most part, inhabitants of "The Bronx" were 18-30 years old. Over time, the Bronx had become a hardcore place where bullets flew every night. Many of the teen boys turned to gangs and people didn't feel as safe as they once had.

"The Vietnam" had a similar makeup, but the heads of households were mostly young adults under 25 years old. This area was a magnet for young thugs who instigated and led violent rages causing the subdivision to be named after one of America's most notorious wars. Fighting initiated from minor issues such as stepping on someone's gym shoes to "turf wars."

"The Circle" and "Eleventh Street" intersected and were a bit mellow because they both still housed families and senior citizens back in the early 1980s. Fifteenth Street was similar to the Circle projects; the senior citizens kept their eyes open for crime and were constantly calling the police to report suspicious activity. Both "The Circle" projects and Fifteenth Street would eventually become two of the hottest drug territories in Ford Heights. Three guys, Big Boo, Lucas, and Kojac established one of the biggest drug operations Ford Heights had ever seen. Along with another guy, Napoleon, they would later be blamed for the introduction of crack cocaine to Ford Heights. I was born and raised on Fifteenth Street.

Chapter 3

The Beginning

I had ants in my pants. It was the second day of preschool and I would get to see all of my new friends again. The sun was shining and I could hardly wait to be dropped off. My brothers had both already started school, they were in the first and second grade. Mama dressed me in a brand new cute bell-bottom pant outfit and pressed my hair straight with a scorching hot straightening comb. I was adorned with cute pink and white ribbons tied around my ponytail, sitting high on the top of my head. The back of my hair hung between my shoulder blades. I was a cute kid and everyone told me so.

I ran into the school to play with my friends. The colorful playground attached to the building was surrounded by a fence for safety. The only way into the park was through the preschool doors. That day, we learned to write our names on paper with wide lines, had nap time, and ate lunch.

After lunch we were allowed to go out and play, but when play time was over I got to stay on the playground a little longer than my classmates. My teacher, Mr. Johns had explained that I'd been *privileged* because I had been a good girl. I slid down the sliding board and fell to the ground, but I didn't cry. I was too happy to be the *only* one allowed to stay outside and play. As I was about to go up the slide again Mr. Johns yelled for me to come over to him. "Why? I wanna go up again!" I replied. "You can go play again soon, just come here first," he said. I walked over to him and he grabbed my hand to pull me closer to him, placing me onto his lap. Mr. Johns rubbed my hair and his large hand trailed across my pink ribbon as he doodled with the bow in my head. He then put both of his hands around my tummy and clasped his hands together. I felt his penis harden as he pulled me back and forth over and over again on his lap, and when he stopped I knew it was over. "Can I go back in and play with my friends now?" Mr. Johns fixed his clothes, stood up and answered, "Yeah, you can go back in now, but don't tell anyone about our secret." I jumped off his lap and shyly dropped my chin toward the ground in embarrassment.

I ran inside the building and never told anyone our secret.

Chapter 4

Mama

My mama was referred to as *high yellow* back in the day. If you fell into the "high yella" category you weren't a dark-skinned black nor were you a brown-skinned black. You were "bright and close to white." It was a common belief that the lighter your complexion the greater the likelihood that at some point in your lineage, the master had *visited* the slave quarters.

Mama's complexion normally would have made her heir to a long list of enemies, but her strong personality and wit was a welcome comfort to black folks and neighbors. The characteristic that separated Mama from white people, as far as the town folk were concerned was her coarse hair and her strong authoritative voice. She was well liked and accepted in our community and she'd proven that she was one of "them." She was indeed a "sistah," strong-willed, fast-talking and a no-jive-taking sistah.

Mama was a "looker." She had a body with curves that made everyone's head turn. Many were enamored with her beauty and loved to see her coming; she was the Lena Horne of the projects. I was born when my mother was only twenty years old, so by the time I was thirteen, Mama was thirty-three, and she still looked twenty-five. Mama was 5'6" with broad shoulders. She wasn't model tall, but her high heels made her appear even more regal than she already was. She was a black woman and proud of it. I was a couple shades darker than my mother, but her spitting image.

By the time my mother was twenty three, she was a single parent with four children. Options for housing were very slim, so we spent most of our childhood living in housing projects. At one time, the projects had been safe, and there were no strangers, we all knew each other. Back then, parents seemed to have a good grip on the children and the old African proverb "It takes a village to raise a child," was valued. Every adult had a hand in raising the neighborhood children in our project community. But, when the neighborhood started to change in the late 1980s, crime had become common place and no one could do anything about it. Drug dealing had replaced the once booming blue collar factory work, which had become non existent.

Drug dealers were earning respect by using violence and the attraction of quick, easy and flashy money to control, manipulate and influence those at the bottom of the totem pole. We were too young and naïve to really understand what was happening around us and the adults seemed oblivious to fast trends that were taking root. Employment would become a thing of the past for most of the adults and it wasn't until later that I'd realize a lot of them couldn't read, including my grandfather.

College was not a table topic in most homes, so families were lucky if their children even made it through high school. Many were caught with no work, no skills, no trades and no degrees. Most turned to drugs as a means to make money and to erase the painful reality that living in the projects was a dead end road. Plain and simple, we knew no other way of life. Everyone around us maintained like minded personas and passed them down through generations. Life outside the confines of public housing was considered unconquerable, and life as we knew it had not provided feasible alternatives to the streets.

Our maze kept us bound within the *invisible fence* surrounding Ford Heights and the projects, forcing us to stay land-locked, mind-locked, and without ambition or a mindset required for an escape.

The impact of television and violent rap songs made selling drugs appear even more glamorous and prosperous. During that time, conflicts between the popular east coast and west coast rappers were fueling a false reality in the hood that heightened drug-selling and violence without the slightest thought of the consequences; death, destruction and its cruel aftermath. Ambulance and police sirens were sounding night after night and traffic on our block had increased. Though these things were happening right under our noses we were *still* children, full of the pure joys that came with the innocence of youth. We played Double Dutch, ate loads of candy, and ran around each other's yard before the street lights came on. We ignored what was going on around us, and were naive to the devastation of the changing environment. The lights, sirens, and gun violence had become the norm of living in our hood and everyone continued in oblivion, as if *this* was normal.

Although we didn't know it, poverty was every where we turned in Ford Heights. People were living without natural gas, electricity, clean clothes and at times, food. Poor people were creative though and it wasn't uncommon to see extension chords running from one project unit to another, providing electricity to a neighbor. When a family's electricity or gas had been disconnected they boiled water to take baths, lit candles to see and used "hot plates" to cook. Unless you lived in the apartment or were related to the affected family there was usually no clue that neighbors lacked these necessities. Mama made sure we had the bare necessities and if a utility was ever disconnected, by evening it was paid and turned back on.

Sometimes I wondered how mama did it. She gave birth to my oldest brother when she was seventeen, my other brother at eighteen, and me at twenty. Four more children were born after me. I would never really know the sacrifices that she made for us. I didn't want to know what her world was like, and I'm sure I didn't have the capacity to understand it at the time. I was a young girl without those kinds of worries whatever "*those*" worries were.

And all we ever heard from adults was to "stay in a child's place" or "it aint for you to worry about," so we continued in our world of naïveté because it was comfortable there.

Mama wasn't real happy when I came home from school one day crying. I'd been teased for the tag that was stapled to the back of my shirt. A classmate had pulled the tag off and ran around the school laughing, "De'Vonna Bentley cost seventy-five cents!" We never knew or cared where most of our clothes came from. Mama was a proud woman; she was never ashamed of our situation and she made the best of her means to provide for us. She never asked any of our fathers for anything and she went on with life, rearing her children and preparing them for real life. I'd heard her say on occasion, "Y'all is my kids and no matter what, I gotta take care 'o ya. I'm not begging no man to take care of his own kids." Not only did mama not beg a man to help with his children, she raised four of us without any support from the men that fathered us. We didn't have all the things we wanted, but we never *felt* poor.

My grandparents were very religious people and all of their children were taught to love God.

Big Daddy was a long time deacon at Peace Missionary Baptist church where he served until the day he died. The church members all raved about how "God had given Deacon Bentley a vision to build the new sanctuary," and though it had taken many years, the beautiful edifice was built with fourteen hundred dollars and unshakeable faith.

Big Mama was one of the "church mothers," responsible for instructing young women and children how to live holy and to uphold the protocols and responsibilities of the church. She had eyes in the back of her head; she'd catch kids walking during the sermon or chewing gum and inflict a motherly look upon the guilty that worked like the worse punishment. She was the church soloist and had a powerful voice like Mahalia Jackson—she stirred up the church with her powerful melodies and soul shaking voice Sunday after Sunday.

Mama didn't go to church much back then because she didn't believe in playing with God. She believed that Christians should live a life that mirrored Christ and if you weren't living that way, you shouldn't be a hypocrite, "all up in church giving God glory with dirty hands."

But, rearing good, respectful children was important to mama and it meant *sending* us to church every Sunday even if she didn't go. This was her way of making certain we didn't become a headache for her later. Everyone always raved about how nice Mama's children dressed and how well behaved we all were. It made her proud because she was able to see the return on her investment. She didn't accept misbehaving from her children and she worked hard to make sure we were all well trained and respectful. She kept all seven of us "in check" and everyone knew it. We didn't get beatings, we got whippings, and there was a big difference. Some of our cousins got beat with extension cords. Mama only had to give us "the look," and if you got a "whipping" you really had it coming.

When my cousin and I were about ten years old, we opened my neighbor's mailbox and destroyed her mail. We laughed, skipped, and sang while throwing the various pieces of mail around the neighborhood. We watched the mail blow away in the wind. There were several pieces that we'd even ripped up! To our dismay, another neighbor had seen us take the mail out of the box.

Before we could make it back to my house my mom and the neighbors were all searching for us! We didn't understand that checks came in the mail and families lived off that check for a whole month. We definitely didn't understand the importance of a Social Security check. We found out that we had ripped up our neighbor's *only* source of income by being mischievous for no reason at all. We were sent on a hunt for the check, but after hours of searching we'd only been able to find three pieces of the Social Security check. Mama was livid and I got the whipping of my life!

When mama wasn't regulating our behavior, she was working part time at "The Velvet." The Velvet was a small bar that had served several generations of families by providing many juke joint type nights with dancing, drinking, and a good ole time! The brick building featured no architectural creativity and was no more than a thousand square feet, and that's being generous. Half of the building was used for the liquor store and snacks, and children often walked in to purchase candy and pop during the day. The remaining footage had a dance floor, bar, and juke box. The place was a hole in the wall but a definite escape from life's problems for a poverty-stricken town.

It didn't matter that the Velvet Room was right across from the police station; the parking lot was a known high-traffic drug area. No IDs were required for entry. Once you were inside The Velvet, you prayed there wasn't a fight or a fire. Other than the side door that was sometimes open to let air in the building there was no other way out. It was very congested, but always crowded because it was easy to get to and located right off a major Highway.

The Ford Stamping Plant was one of the last major factories in Ford Heights with no signs of leaving. The employees met daily at The Velvet for happy hour and their patronage helped to secure The Velvet's existence for years to come.

Mama worked day shifts as a nursing assistant, then she'd come home to nap, cook dinner, clean and then go to work at The Velvet until closing time at four o'clock in the morning. Mama worked sixteen hours days three to four days a week, but still managed to keep a sparkling clean apartment. People didn't understand how she did it with seven children.

In the summer, mama cooked large pots of pasta and tuna salads for dinner so we'd have leftovers. We ate spiced ham and bologna for lunch on the days mama worked. She sent us to Dejulio Corner Store with food stamps and we'd buy pounds of spiced ham. We ate spiced ham for days at a time. We fried spiced ham, rolled spice ham, cut it into tiny pieces, and ate it raw. And eventually when we didn't want to see spiced ham any more it became a weapon; we threw it at each other!

There were times when Mama would come home from The Velvet and we didn't have food for breakfast. She'd either been too busy to go to the grocery store or had been working long hours. After ransacking the cupboards in hopes of finding something that didn't need to be cooked, we were left disappointed. The girls were always given the task of crawling into mama's room and waking her up at eight o'clock in the morning. We knew better than to show up any earlier, when she'd just gotten in at four o'clock a.m.

"Mama, we're out of cereal and milk," we'd tell her.

She would reach into her bra, pull out a wad of money or food stamps, depending on the time of the month, and proceed to make a list of things we needed.

Then, she'd roll over and go back to sleep, but not before she gave us that *look,* "Make sure yall bring me back all my change." Before we headed to the store, we usually begged mama to allow us to purchase the three flavor coconut slice candy she loved. And more times than not, mama gave in. She didn't allow us to eat lots of candy, so whenever we did get it, we knew it was a treat.

Most of us kids were happy to have food stamps, and to us, they were better than dollar bills. Back then we didn't know if you received food stamps you were poor. There was no real way to know that we were poor because for the most part our household ran smoothly. Mama worked mostly everyday, she paid the bills, and she provided our every *need.*

It was always an adventure watching mama assemble her outfit and get dressed for work at The Velvet. My sisters and I admired her; she had so much style and pizzazz. When she wasn't home, we tried on her shoes, clothes, and her jewelry and took turns pretending that we were "Julie Ann Bentley". Watching her, I'd imagine an artist painting a picture.

She was very methodical and we learned early that you didn't just walk out of the house looking undone; you had to have yourself together. One of mama's favorite sayings was, "People *see* you before they *know* you, so you got to look good at all times."

With her hair fresh from the Jheri curl and streaks of blonde, she'd grab a pair of skinny jeans, put on lipstick, mascara, and dab perfume behind her neck. Then she grabbed her three-and-a-half-inch heels from the stairs and we knew it was a done deal. The painting was complete and what a masterpiece it was. Mama was on her way to The Velvet and we'd still be sleeping when she returned from her shift.

Shortly after Mama started working at The Velvet she bought a shiny blue Cutlass Supreme and it was evident that we were doing better. People started to speculate where her money was coming from and those things rumors filtered down through their children. Mama came home one day and I couldn't look at her, when she asked what was wrong with me I burst into tears. I was embarrassed and didn't want to tell her why I was so upset.

"Girl, you better tell me why you crying!" she demanded. Mama was stern, but she had the face of an angel. I sobbed between words and told her that my classmates had said "She was a prostitute and everyone knew it." Mama laughed, "Girl, what are you talking about? You don't let nobody tell you nothing about me. Do you think I'm a prostitute?" Suddenly I was quieted by my mother's reprimanding gaze. I felt as small as I was, "No, Mama, I don't think you are a pra-pra-pra-sti-tute." I was ashamed to repeat the word. "Okay then, people is going to talk about you until the day you die." From that day forward, no one could tell me anything about my mama.

One day she came home from her day job and excitedly loaded us kids into the car; she had a surprise for us. Mama drove two blocks from our apartment and stopped in front of an unoccupied *shack* not far from where we lived. She pulled a key out of her purse and got out of the car. Once she opened the door and cleared a path inside, she yelled for us to get out and come in. We got out of the car and followed mama inside. The building was small, had a stove, kitchen, and three tables for customers eating in.

The walls were freshly painted and still reeked of paint and it was evident that much of the work had recently taken place. There was still work to be done when mama excitedly announced to us that *Henry's Rib Joint* would be opening in two weeks! She had rented the space and turned it into a barbecue joint and named it after my grandfather. The rib joint had become our hang out and we were seeing Mama more often. It was the new spot for good food and great socializing and when it wasn't busy we'd go there and do homework or help mama.

We knew things were getting better for us financially and it was different from the "better" that we'd experienced when Mama worked at The Velvet. The feeling of ownership gave us something we could be proud of, but the feeling was short lived and only lasted a few months. Mysteriously, Henry's Rib Joint burned down one night, and like most business owners during that time, Mama didn't have renters insurance. She wasn't able to open the business again and had to go back to working at The Velvet. She wasn't happy about it, but she knew she could make quick money and would always have cash to provide for the things we needed.

While working at The Velvet, Mama met my stepfather Ron. He had recently moved to Ford Heights from Memphis, Tennessee and they quickly became an item. When mama introduced Ron to us we all liked him, but we thought it was funny that he always wore a suit and a tie. My younger sister and I laughed at how much Ron looked like Lionel Richie. He was tall, perfectly slim and had smooth medium brown skin. We all agreed that he looked like a black Ken doll. No matter what the occasion or the day of the week, Ron wore his church clothes. He'd walk into a room with his suit, tie, and dress shoes on. Men in our neighborhood only wore suits and ties on Sunday morning. Mama and Ron started spending a lot of time together so we knew she liked him. She'd never brought a man around us before.

There was no formal announcement, but as their relationship progressed, we realized he had become a resident in our home. Mama trusted him so we knew we could trust him too. Although we never verbalized it we were all proud to finally have a "daddy" in our house. My stepfather was a good, hardworking man.

He provided for us in every way that a father was expected, and when he got home in the afternoon he cooked dinner. On the weekends he cooked a southern style breakfast with biscuits, bacon, eggs, and grits. We lived for the Sunday meals Ron cooked. His famous gravy smothered rabbit, rice, and collard greens were delectable, and our mouth watered for his cooking. With Ron in the house, mama didn't have to cook and we didn't mind it at all. He never talked much, but we all knew he loved us in his own way; his actions spoke volumes. He cooked, cleaned, went to work, and watched baseball. He had a nice, shiny car and worked every day. When we got up for school each morning, Ron would already be gone because he left for work at four o'clock every morning. He'd even leave money on the dresser for us if we had stuff going on at school. Ron and my mother conceived three children, China, Shanece, and Ron Jr., but most days, mama and Ron were like two ships passing in the night. He'd be leaving for work and mama would just be coming home.

After several years, mama and Ron decided to go their separate ways. Just as there had been no formal announcement when Ron moved in, there wasn't one when he moved out. After their separation, mama and Ron still spent time together and often went out in public as if they were still together. We all missed his presence in the house, but eventually their relationship ended all together and it didn't change how Ron interacted with each of us. After he moved out, he sent mama an envelope filled with cash each week.

Although it wasn't the same as having a father in the house, having two older brothers relieved the feelings of being fatherless. Bryce and Eric had become our protectors. Bryce was a hot head from birth. I guess he had to be that way because Mama was single and he was always in charge when she wasn't home. Eric was the peacemaker, calm and clear-headed, the total opposite of Bryce.

I was number three of seven children. Mama said that she'd prayed for me, and when she found out she had given birth to a daughter, it was "divine," so I was endowed with a French name, De'Vonna, which means "divine."

I loved growing up in a house with a lot of kids, and Mama enjoyed it too. She had thirteen siblings, and I think it reminded her of her own childhood. There were always kids in our house which made it hard to keep track of everything that was going on there. As far as the adults were concerned, survival was more important than anything else. Every day was another day for parents to figure out how to make it through. Mama would often say, "Lord, thank you for today's portion." Thinking back, it's easy to understand why things that were happening in the projects went unnoticed for many years.

Chapter 5

Let the Games Begin

My mother yelled upstairs for us to be ready in twenty minutes. We were all frantically running around trying to figure out which toys we would take to my aunt's house. She was having a card game and it wasn't just a card game to pass time. They gambled for money. The usual people would be there, my aunts, uncles, close friends of the family, and people that heard there would be big money at the table. Many of the players didn't have high paying jobs and some weren't employed at all, so the stakes were high.

Sometimes the card games would last for days extending through the entire weekend. Those games were fun for us because it meant we'd see other kids that we normally didn't get to see, but we hated going to the card games at my aunt's house because there was no entertainment. She didn't even have a television in her living room, so we were forced to bring toys and school work. We knew when we got there we'd have to be creative.

Once we got there, I pulled out the paper dolls that I'd sketched, colored, and cut out, along with clothes that I'd made for them. Tabs were located on the shoulders and the waist of each outfit and would easily bend over the paper doll to stay in place. I usually got paper dolls for Christmas, but when they were worn out, I resorted to making my own. I made perfect paper dolls with perfect clothes. I had books to read and my paper dolls, so I definitely would not be bored. I made sure to have more than enough to keep me busy while we were there.

Though the maximum number of six players had been reached, many adults were still standing around the table waiting to play Six Card Rum. It was a packed house and people would be coming and going all night long waiting for their opportunity to play! Everyone in my neighborhood played Six Card Rum, even the children. Whenever I stayed overnight at my grandparent's house, my cousins and I would wake up early, climb trees, play in the park, and wait for the neighborhood children to wake up. We'd sit on the concrete in broad daylight and gamble. Yes we did!

Many times we'd have other children waiting to gamble too. Our stakes weren't as high as the adults, but a nickel was a lot of money back then. If there were six kids playing, the winner walked away with thirty cents! Usually it was spent at Ms. Bertha Lee's, "the candy store house." We loved spending our money on the chic-o-sticks, lemon heads, freezer cups, baked beans, and penny candies, it made gambling worth it.

"Put me up," my aunt requested of my mom. By the sixth hand she was broke and had lost her entire paycheck and would not be getting paid for another week. It was not unusual for an adult to lose every dime they had playing cards. They played a game of chance and would leave empty-handed. If a player wasn't smart enough to quit when the getting was good, they were definitely going home broke because there could only be one winner.

"This is the last time I'm putting you up," my mother declared as she sternly gazed into my aunt's eyes, but she didn't have to worry. My aunt won the next hand and was back in the game. Some would leave happy and others would most definitely leave distraught! Feeding the kids after losing was a whole 'nother' battle.

Those that lost had to work a full week or wait an entire month for a welfare check before they could buy food. There were times when the big winner was merciful and loaned money to the biggest loser, so they could at least feed their children.

On occasion, the adults considered me the entertainment at the card games and during intermission; I'd be their showcase of talent. I was an early reader and all the adults got a kick out of having me read. That made mama so proud.

"De'Vonna, come on in here, baby," she'd yell. I'd been beckoned to the dining room where the adults were all sitting around. The other children trailed behind me as I proudly walked into the kitchen. I'd been sight-reading words since before I could put a sentence together "sit, run, car."

My mother would excitedly remind her friends, "That girl been reading since before she could talk. She was reading the Enfamil cans and cereal boxes. She reads like a LOCOMOTIVE!" She would then break out into a hysterical, gut-wrenching laugh. When she was able to contain herself she'd say, "Read girl." Mama was bent over in her seat laughing as she motioned through her laughter,"Teach these grown folks how to read."

That was my cue, I'd stand up straight, find my place in my book, and zoom through the words. When I stopped reading, all the adults would laugh and clap in amazement. My mom would smile and proudly excuse me back to the living room to play with my paper dolls.

Chapter 6

What's Done in the Dark

Oh, the stairs. I remember the stairs, there were twelve of them. Each stair was perfectly covered with a strip of rubber to prevent slips or falls. I had fun running up and down those stairs, seeing my mama's shoes lined up on each step, and listening to grown folks conversations from the top of those stairs. I couldn't wait to be a grownup so I could wear the four-inch heels that mama wore. I was going to line my stairs with shoes too.

As a young girl, I enjoyed standing at the top of the stairs and imagining that I was on the highest mountain in the world. My siblings and I would slide down the stairs when mama hosted card parties to try to get as close to the action as we could. The music was timeless back then. We loved hearing the powerful vocals of Chaka Khan, Lenny Williams, Luther Vandross, and all the great R & B artists...

Mama was hosting a card party and we heard the music blasting through the speakers as we played on the stairs.

We weren't allowed to hang out downstairs or hear the gossip firsthand, but once I overheard the first good story. I'd leap from the top of the stairs until I reached the bottom step. Then, I'd peak around the corner to investigate who had made it to the party so far.

The music resonated throughout our apartment, smoke floated up the stairs from cigarettes, and mama's friends were talking, laughing, and drinking. It was about to be a good time. As I sat on the stairs one of my cousins reached down into my shirt and grabbed my breast. I shrieked and before I knew it, my hand fell hard onto the back of his neck as he tried to run off. I jumped up and yelled to my mother, hoping that my voice would reach the bottom of the stairs and float into the kitchen. When mama didn't hear me, I ran down the stairs and stopped at the final step. I knew not to go any further. I repeated, "Mama, Jeff touched my chest, and he being nasty!" Mama had heard me both times and said she would soon come up to find out what was going on. She'd had enough of us, and I knew if I continued to make these *accusations* she would be on her way upstairs to whip me.

I stomped up the stairs irritated because it had been the truth. We had been disrupting the card game for hours, running up and down, sliding down the stairs, singing loudly, and screaming to bring attention to ourselves. Mama had company and she had to watch her money. When an adult hosted a card party, it meant much more than opening up their home for people to gamble and to have a good time. They had a responsibility to the event; they were in charge of buying liquor, cooking food, and inviting people who would pay to play. There were usually six players, and the host collected the proceeds from one player for every round that was dealt. That was their "cut." Each player placed ten or twenty dollars on the table depending on the amount they were gambling for. The winner's proceeds were fifty to one hundred dollars per game and the host would get ten to twenty dollars per hand. If mama paid attention, she could walk away with hundreds of dollars from a card game just for hosting, and we would all reap the benefits of her "come up." The card game had ended, but my cousins were still at our house and would stay through the weekend.

Chapter 7

The Unknown Infestation

Projects had cockroaches. It was a well known fact. It didn't matter if your project unit was clean or dirty. If your neighbor had them, so did you. They hid in cracks and crevices, and late at night they came out and crawled around on the countertops. Cockroaches were simply a common and persistent problem in the projects that we all hated and wished would go away. As soon as the lights were turned on, the roaches sought refuge in dark spaces. Cockroaches weren't the only things lurking at night, there was an *unknown infestation* happening all around us.

During the day, I'd enjoy the hot weather just like the other girls, I played Double Dutch and laughed and giggled with all the other kids. When dusk set we'd catch lightening bugs; we'd pull out the glowing part of the tail, and place the neon substance on our ears. All the girls walked around at night with "glow earrings" on. When the sun went down and all the shades were drawn, there were things going on in our apartment that people didn't know about. Mama didn't even know.

One particular night, my mom had agreed to let my cousin Jeff spend the night. I was lying in my bed and awakened by someone who had come into my bedroom and climbed into my bed. I could feel this person inching closer to me until there was no space left between us. My mother was working and my sisters had been quietly sleeping in the bunk bed and the other twin bed in the room we all shared.

Jeff crawled on top of me and began moving his body up and down. He put his hands around my waist and pulled me closer to him. He began "grinding" on me with his clothes on, moaning and making noises that I had heard only on television. When he was done he slid out of my bed and disappeared down the hallway, back into my brothers' bedroom.

Mama often allowed my cousins to stay at our house overnight, but she had no idea what was going on while she was at work, or even on some nights when she was home sleeping. If Mama had known what was going on they would have never been welcomed in our home. But how could I tell her? I couldn't tell anyone. It was shameful and I feared being the subject of town gossip.

I'd heard the familial gossip about my cousin who had been molested by an uncle. It was swept under the rug and never spoken of outside the family. Some had even suggested that she probably wanted it. 'How could they think she was at fault?' I wondered. I'd felt bad for her and even though I knew what was happening to me, I made a promise to myself that I would not endure the same agony. I would not have people looking at me strangely and talking behind my back. I could not sign up for that. What my uncle had done to her was wrong. She'd gotten pregnant and the family pretended it never happened. 'No, I definitely couldn't tell anyone.'

The overnight visits by my cousins always meant that someone would be tiptoeing into my bedroom at some point during the night. One thing I knew for certain was that this was wrong. I had to stop it, but I didn't know how or who I could trust to tell. Over time, the incidents escalated from simple grinding with clothes on, to skin contact. I learned to trick them into believing they were having sex with me.

They would lay on top of me after crawling into my bed and fondle my tiny breasts and eventually raise my gown and stick their penis between my legs. With every muscle in my body, I would close my legs as tight as I could to make them believe that they were inside me. When that familiar feeling of a climax occurred I knew that I had once again outfoxed them. When they crawled out of my bedroom, I repeatedly told myself that 'It was a dream and that my body, mind, and soul were never there.' It didn't matter because they still had no idea that they had not actually been having sex with me. There had been no penetration and I'd felt relieved when they were done because I had been able to protect my "cherry." That's what I had heard my aunts and the older ladies around me call it. "You'd better make sure you don't give up that cherry," so I was proud of it and I protected *it*.

No matter what the circumstance, I would never let that happen. Nope, not me, and not by one of my cousins! I had it all figured out until my cousin Damien crawled into my bedroom. Damien was heavier than I, but I was ready. I was going to pretend we were having sex.

I would do my usual close-my-legs-tight-and-wait-until-he-climaxed trick. I knew it would be a little challenging due to his weight, but just as I had with my other cousins, I'd pretend that he was inside me and it would be over in no time. Damien pulled his pants down, got on top of me, and placed his penis between my thighs. I could feel the hardness of it as I pressed my legs closer together as I'd done with my other cousins. As he maneuvered his body on top of mine, I knew that he was not getting the satisfaction that he sought. He began to get closer to my private area and I knew he was definitely on a different mission; he was looking for complete fulfillment. I tried to stay focused on what I had become accustomed to as I shifted my body from side to side.

'Yes, that's it, he won't know the difference,' I thought. If I could just shift a little, I would be safe like I'd been with my other cousins, but I was seriously worried because Damien was *different*. He had figured out quickly that he wasn't really having sex with me and tried to pry my legs open. I squeezed my legs closer together, but my muscles were weak and my strength was no match for him.

My eyes filled with tears. I wished someone would come into the bedroom at that moment. I quickly rethought that. 'No! I didn't want anyone to come in now.' I didn't want my younger sisters to wake up to find him on top of me. No, that wouldn't be good! No matter the sacrifice, I would not allow anyone to catch him on top of me. I kept repeating the same scenario in my head of how everyone would judge me and say bad things about me. I could hear the words consistently being repeated in my head "Little fass tail." These words were used loosely in my neighborhood and the common phrase had begun to lose its original intended meaning. At one time fass meant "fast." If a girl was sexually active, promiscuous, or dressed provocative, she was considered *fass*. Now, everyone seemed to fall within that category. If your hips started forming, you were fass. If you were cute, you were fass. If your breasts started to grow, you were fass. If you showed emotion, you were fass. 'Yeah, she wanted it. Look how she be acting, her fass ass!' That's what they would all think of me. They would think I was being fass. I was afraid that if I made too much noise someone would come into the room and accuse me of being fass.

I didn't want anyone to think I was fass so I didn't scream. 'Did I deserve what was happening to me? Is this what fass girls got?' I asked myself. My best friend's mother had said I was fass. My grandmother and aunts had all called me fass. I could not prove them right, so I would keep my mouth closed and get through this because this is what fass girls got.

Tears continued to fall when I thought of how sick it would be for someone to ever think I wanted this to happen. Who would ever want *this* to happen? I realized that this was the worst day of my life as my twelve-year-old body lay there helpless with him on top of me about to rob me of everything I'd ever tried to protect. I had made the decision not to scream. It wasn't worth it. I was done wishing that someone would have come in and caught him crawling into my bedroom that night because it was too late. I was an accomplice.

That night things changed, and I quickly realized he knew more about sex than the others did. He was forceful and experienced, and he knew exactly how to find my vagina. I could tell that he meant business, but I had to protect my cherry. I wanted to scream, but I couldn't let anyone know what was happening.

I shrieked as I felt his penis pressing against me. "No, we can't do this!" He was larger than I was and continued to press harder against me. "What are you doing?" I whispered repeatedly. "Stop now before I scream," I said. My urging him to stop only seemed to give him power. I knew in my heart that I wouldn't scream, but I wanted him to stop. As he pulled at my underwear I imagined everyone's accusatory tone, "It was your fault! You should have told someone." He was aggressive, and knew exactly what he wanted, his plan was to penetrate me. Damien forced my legs open and I struggled to stop him. He grabbed both of my wrists and held my hands over my head as tight as he could with one hand as I pleaded for him to stop.

I had concocted a plan to protect my cherry -- I'd started sleeping in pajama pants because I thought if I was wearing pants there would be no penetration, but tonight I'd worn a gown and Damien knew just how to get to my cherry. He rubbed his hard penis against my inner thigh, and his breathing became hot and heavy. He was sweating from the struggle that I was putting up and I could feel him fighting his way in. I was helpless in my own home, in the bedroom that I shared with my younger sisters.

He pried my legs open and forced his penis inside my vagina. Tears streamed down the side of my face. "No, nooooo noooo!" He had taken it. My cherry. As his breathing intensified, something assured me that it would be over soon. I imagined being outside jumping Double Dutch with my friends, playing Chinese jacks and Hide-and-Go-Seek. I was lying under my fifteen-year-old cousin, and without a sense of emotion, the battle between me, my life, and what I wanted to protect had been lost. I had heard from older girls that they had gotten their cherries popped and it felt good. They'd liked it, and wanted more, but I didn't like it, and didn't want more. The games were over, and it had happened just like that. I had not been able to pretend with him and I'd gotten my cherry popped. I cried from the piercing pain as his penis slid in and out of my vagina in painful, pounding thrusts. I counted in my head. It would be over soon...100....99...98....97......96.....95...This was much worse than when my uncle had given me beer and fondled my breasts while babysitting us because, well, he'd given us beer, and all kids want to taste beer.

Every time he babysat us he'd either have a girlfriend over and take her in Mama's room and close the door or he'd sneak into our room and slide into the bottom bunk with me and touch my developing breasts. At that time, my uncle was twenty years old and I was eleven. He'd lie on top of me and move back and forth, up and down until he climaxed. He never touched my cherry. I think he was too worried that I'd tell my mother, and he calculated the risks. Damien hadn't calculated the risks. Somehow I'd told myself that since my uncle didn't have sex with me, I didn't have to tell on him. Besides, when Mama wasn't there he let us stay outside a little longer. Mama always made us come in when the streetlights came on. All of our friends would be outside playing, and we'd be looking out the window wishing we were outside too. Uncle let us stay out late.

I continued to count...20....19....18....17....16....15...14, and finally he rolled over onto his side. He was finished. I was emotionless as Damien slid onto the floor and crawled out of my bedroom quietly.

I hadn't wanted this to happen. I'd only played a game up until this point. But he had forced himself on me, and I couldn't tell anyone. I would never tell a soul. I would pretend it never happened. But I knew it did because I'd replayed the scene over and over in my head, and I was reminded that I was no longer pure. I wanted to hate him. I wanted to hate myself, but I couldn't. I didn't.

No one heard a thing – or at least I don't think they did. I wondered if the same things had happened to my sisters. I wondered if it was just a nasty thing that happened in the ghetto, in the projects – a nasty secret that we didn't talk about. Maybe it had happened to mama and her sisters and my friends and their sisters and my aunts and grandmothers. Maybe this had just become a horrible tradition passed down through generations that no one talked about. I just couldn't bring myself to believe nor did I want to believe that I was the only one who endured the physical, psychological, and emotional pain of sexual abuse.

Something was dripping from my vagina. 'Was this the first symptom of a popped cherry?' Suddenly I remembered what I had heard in sex education class. 'Oh my God, I'm pregnant!' My mother was going to kill me. No one would feel sorry for me and they would all hate me for getting pregnant. The pain was excruciating, and I contemplated touching *it* to ease the pain. Touching it would be *nasty*. Instead, I placed my hand on my thigh and wept and I hoped my vagina would get the message 'I was sorry that this had happened, so very sorry.' The pain reverberated. My vagina was sore and swollen, but I managed to pull myself out of bed after putting my underwear back on. It hurt to walk, but I got to the bathroom and stood there looking in the mirror. I cried. By then it was after three o'clock in the morning. I hated myself. I hated this life that I'd been born into. I dug my fingernails deep into my face as I cursed the day I was born. I wished I was so ugly that no one would look at me. I wished I could walk into a room and not get any attention. I didn't want any one to notice me. I wanted to be invisible. Why did I have to be *pretty*? This had all happened because I was *pretty*?

The compliments. My cousins. The projects. My life. They had all begun to remind me of something utterly disgusting. All these things reminded me of the roaches that scattered when lights were turned on. After they had spent an evening feasting, leeching, and snatching crumbs off the counter, they ran from the light. There was nothing more disgusting than that. *The roaches had started to multiply.*

I had to clean myself up before anyone got up. We had one bathroom and I didn't want anyone to become suspicious of me being in the bathroom for an extended period. I looked down at my soiled underwear and continued to silently weep. There was blood and other fluids in my underwear.

'Why was I even born, God? Why did this happen to me? If you really loved me, God, why did you allow this to happen to me?' What would I tell Mama? She did all of the laundry so she would definitely see the blood in my underwear. I'd have to tell her that I had started my period. Yes. That would be the excuse for the blood! I took my panties off and filled the sink with water to let them soak just long enough to lift the stubborn blood stains. I needed to get as much of the blood out as I could.

I rubbed the bar of soap against the cotton underwear and scrubbed as hard as I could. The stains were stubborn and didn't seem to want to come out. I scrubbed harder and harder!

If…I…could…only…get…all…of…the…blood…out…. it…would…be…easier…to…pretend….that…thissss… nevvver…..happened. I scrubbed until my hands hurt. I couldn't allow Mama or anyone else to find blood in my panties! I scrubbed for dear life. I scrubbed to forget my uncle lying on top of me. I scrubbed to forget my preschool teacher. I scrubbed to forget my cousin. I could survive this, I knew I could. I had to. I scrubbed to forget the fluids that were still dripping from my throbbing vagina. I scrubbed until I began to forget what had happened tonight. There! Every speck of blood had come out.

Tonight, nothing happened…

Chapter 8

An Epidemic

Incest ran deep in my family -- deeper than anyone dared to admit. Family members whispered about the things that happened within other family members' homes. And though many of the rumors were true, they were never reported to the police or muttered outside the realm of family.

My grandmother, at five feet eight inches, deserved the name Big Mama because she was a hefty woman, large in size and stature. My grandfather was a very quiet man, but we feared him the way we feared God. He stood right at my grandmother's shoulder; they were just about the same height. Though he was an average sized man, we called him Big Daddy anyway.

He was very loving, but didn't talk much. He doted over every child, grandchild, and great-grandchild. Although he was reserved, he would lash out only in the most critical moments. If Big Daddy spanked you, it was for something really bad.

When he found out about what my uncle had done, he beat him with a baseball bat and threatened to kill him.

I remember walking into my grandparents' house a few days after the truth of my cousin's pregnancy had been uncovered. My grandfather was visibly grieved by what had happened and the silence was odd. We weren't used to this kind of quiet in our grandparent's home. When my uncle got my cousin pregnant she'd been living with my grandparents and was only fourteen years old. My grandparents did not believe in abortion so the baby was born six months later. Although my grandparents didn't condone what had happened, their pride would not allow them to become subjects of public ridicule. They were respected in the community by many, and most of the children in Ford Heights called them Big Mama and Big Daddy too, it was as if they were grandparents to the town. They couldn't allow that secret to get out, so we went along with our lives, and we all pretended it never happened.

Molestation didn't just happen in my house; it was happening all around me in the projects, and probably in the suburbs where middle class black folks lived and where the white folks lived too.

Of course we didn't have any dealings with middle class families so I couldn't know for sure.

My best friend Betsy and I spent a lot of time giggling and talking on her front porch. Mostly we talked about the silly boys in our neighborhood. She was a year older, but she was the one girl that understood me. She was pudgy and the boys called her "funny looking." I hated when they teased Betsy about how she looked.

I'd gone to visit Betsy constantly for over a week during the summer, but she never seemed to be home. One day she knocked on my door and said, "My mama said I can't play with you anymore." I didn't understand. We had been best friends longer than we'd both been on the earth and I couldn't remember a day without Betsy. Our mothers were two of the first inhabitants of Fifteenth Street, so she and I had played together for as long as I could remember. The words escaped her mouth, and she showed no remorse. It was settled. We would not be friends anymore. I cried myself to sleep that evening. I had no idea why her mom had made that decision, so I sent letters by Betsy's cousin demanding an explanation because I had done nothing wrong and I missed her.

Betsy finally sent me a response by her cousin, I opened the tattered letter that she'd sent and began to read, it was short and to the point, "My mama said that you is too fass, and I told her that you not, but she don't believe me." I didn't know what made her mother think I was fass. I wasn't. I didn't even like boys. All I wanted to do was make pretend food. Betsy and I had been preparing meals for days from mud and grass. We were going to serve mud pies and greens, but her mom put an end to all of that and I hated her for it. And then, a few months later my mom revealed to me that she'd found out that Betsy was pregnant. I realized that her mother didn't want me to find out that Betsy had gotten pregnant! She was thirteen when she gave birth to her son. He was born with a mental defect.

Without Betsy I was lost and I was in a daze for most of the summer, until I started hanging out with Sandra. I was so excited to have a new best friend. Her mom had been living with her stepfather for years, and they were nice people. There were always cars backed up trying to get into our cul-de-sac to get to Sandra's house. Rumor had it that her parents were selling marijuana.

Mama was very strict and rarely allowed us to visit anyone. Sandra's mom was more lenient and she even allowed us to sit in Sandra's bedroom and talk.

Mama didn't allow kids to sit in our bedrooms and it definitely had to be a blue moon surfacing for her to allow someone to spend the night at our house. We had plenty of cousins, so mama didn't really let people stay overnight unless they were family.

"There are enough of y'all to be friends with each other. Y'all don't need extra kids over here," she said. My younger sister and I shared bunk beds before the arrival of our younger sisters. Eventually there were four girls in one bedroom. Mama was right; we didn't have room for other kids in our house.

Sandra was tiny for her age, had a beautiful caramel complexion, long ponytails, and she was an attractive kid. She appeared very timid, but she was far from timid. She had a potty mouth and kept me in stitches from laughing so hard. It was rare that I heard kids using foul language back then, but Sandra was good at it. When she was angry she would lash out and give someone a verbal whipping that could rupture an ego for weeks.

I was glad I was her best friend because I would never feel her wrath. Regardless of our age difference, we were inseparable. Sandra was pretty too, so I couldn't help but wonder if boys crept into her bedroom at night. We lived in a cul-de-sac right across from each other. We religiously woke up early in the morning, looked out our front windows and waved to each other from our front windows. Eventually she'd end up standing outside my bedroom window yelling, "Ask your mom if you can come outside." We lived to see each other every day. We were two peas in a pod.

My mother didn't allow her kids to go outside before noon. All the other kids would be outside playing and having a good time, but all seven of us would be in the house staring out the window. Sometimes Mama would yell at us to "get out the window looking homeless and find something to do around the house." When the clock struck twelve we'd already made sure that all of our chores were done. The appointed person would be responsible for asking mama if it was now okay for us to go outside to play. Sandra would be waiting for me; she'd already knocked on the door two or more times by then.

"Ms. Julie, can De'Vonna come out and play?" Sandra had asked the same question many times before and mama's answer never changed, "Now Sandra, you know my kids don't come out until noon."

There were other girls on our block, but the girls that lived in our cul-de-sac on Fifteenth Street were close. Angel lived kitty corner from me, and she was one of the sweetest girls on the block. All of the adults in her home were alcoholics. Every day there was a fight going on in her apartment and we witnessed most of the yelling, screaming, and ambulance occurrences. Inevitably, we'd witness someone walking out of her apartment later that week wearing bandages on some part of their body. One day we waited for Angel to come out and play, but there hadn't been a peep from her house at all that day. We later found out that the night before, her grandmother had stabbed her uncle and they'd all gone to the hospital. These kinds of things happened on a regular basis in Angel's home. Angel's uncle survived the stabbing, and eventually she came home and things were back to her "normal". She never talked about what went on in her apartment, but someone was always on the way to the hospital or on the way back.

There were many crazy things happening in our neighborhood and we were conditioned to believe that those things were normal, even if it meant pretending those things never happened.

An aging woman and her thirty-something year old son lived a few houses down from us. The son purposely waited for children to walk by his back door, so he could flash them. He opened his robe and showed his penis on a regular basis. We were told not to walk past his house and to always take the long way home, but they lived right across from the junior high school and some children had to walk by.

There was always some kind of chaos or dysfunction occurring on our street, but the adults and children went on with life as if all were perfect. There were too many other things to worry about. And, we had heard it enough from the adults around us, "It ain't your business, stay out of it," so we did. We went on with our childhood and played Double Dutch for hours unless someone brought Chinese Jacks to break the monotony.

Sandra and I were Double Dutch partners almost every time. Angel was phenomenal at jumping too and on the mornings that I couldn't go outside, she and Sandra would be partners. I hated those mornings. I kept thinking Angel would steal my best friend. That never happened because Sandra and I swore to always be best friends; our promise would bind us together forever and it would ensure that no one would ever come between us. Our promise to love and protect each other began with a secret…

Sandra had something to tell me, and had wanted to tell me her secret all week long, but my siblings and I had been on lockdown because someone had stolen money from Mama and no one would confess. Mama said she was going to give the guilty party some time to decide if they wanted to confess and if no one came forward everyone would have to suffer the consequences. We were all going to be on punishment for the rest of the weekend. It was going to be a long weekend for the four of us older kids because it was summer and all the other kids in the neighborhood would be right outside our window playing.

As the hours went by, Mama assured us that she was no longer mad about the money, but now she was upset that someone was lying. Mama hated a liar. My face had been red from crying and pleading with my siblings to "just tell who did it," but no one gave in. They feared they would get stuck in the house all alone. Whenever we were all in the house we could make it fun. Mama had a soft spot though, and I knew she felt bad about making the innocent ones stay in for something that one or maybe two of the children were guilty of.

When Mama gave in and finally let us outside, Sandra was waiting for me! "I'm so glad you're out of solitary confinement. Girl, Ms. Julie don't be playing with y'all." She was about to burst from the secret she'd been dying to tell me and couldn't hold it in any longer.

"Well, I really want to tell you something, but I don't think you can keep this a secret." I knew this had to be good because she was making a big deal out of it, so I couldn't answer any other way, "I can. I can. I won't tell anyone," I promised.

"I'll tell you on one condition," she said. "I'm not giving you my skirt!" I snapped and attempted to rise up from the sidewalk where we had been sitting. She loved my black faux leather "Tina-Turner-skirt," and had been asking to borrow it for weeks. It wasn't as if she could fit my clothes because I was an average sized kid and she definitely wasn't. Pictures of Tina Turner and her wonderful long legs had made this fashionable skirt very popular! Most of the girls in my neighborhood had all been *sacrificially gifted* with a pleather skirt because our mothers knew how much we loved it.

"No, silly, sit back down," she said. "I need to make sure this stays between us. We are best friends, right?" she asked. "Yes," I said as I slowly sat back down looking sharply at her, wondering what could be so serious. "Well, *now* we are going to be blood sisters, but only if you promise to keep this secret."

"Okay, okay, I will. I promise." I agreed to keep quiet. Sandra jumped up from the pavement where we had been sitting, as if it was an afterthought, and yelled, "I will be right back!"

I waited patiently as Sandra rushed into her house to get the tools that we would need to seal the deal. That day we became *blood sisters* and we made a pact to forever keep this secret, and all others between the two of us. We pricked our index fingers with a sewing needle, rubbed them together, and sucked each other's blood.

After we finished the ritual, she confessed that the handsome twenty-something year old boarder that had been renting a room from her parents had been having sex with her for over three weeks. I gasped, "You have to tell someone! You cannot keep letting this happen!" I envisioned the few times I'd seen the cool boarder. He was tall and handsome just as she had described. He had big eyes that demanded your attention.

I thought back to the time I'd sat in her living room listening to the new Michael Jackson album that he bought her and I remembered his beautiful smile. 'How could he?' I was suddenly angry. Then, I remembered what had happened to me and that I hadn't told a soul, not even Sandra. Even after we became blood sisters I hadn't told her my secrets. I pushed those thoughts out of my mind. "You must tell your mother!" I pleaded with her.

I was a hypocrite. I had tried to persuade her to reveal what was happening in her house because I thought if she divulged her secret we would both be free. She reminded me of the pact we had just made. I was stunned, but I had been sworn to secrecy.

I wouldn't be free today, at least not by her admission. She would tell no one but me about what was occurring in her apartment—right across the street from where my own *stuff* was taking place, and I'd carry my secrets to my grave. I shut my mouth and thought about the disgusting roaches that continued to multiply and I could feel them crawling on my skin.

Chapter 9

What Kind of Love is this?

I'd been sent home from school because I was sick and had thrown up a few times. Mama was concerned about me and though we lived within eyeshot of the junior high school she wouldn't let me walk home sick. Mama drove to school to pick me up, but what she didn't know was that I'd left for school that morning earlier than usual so I could walk with my cousins Jeff and Jay. That morning they dared me to drink Mad Dog 20/20 and I took the dare. I went on to school as if nothing happened, but after about two hours, I began to throw up violently. No one ever knew I was drunk, other than my cousins, who later laughed and called me a lightweight. Mama made me a bowl of soup and took good care of me that evening. I loved the attention, but I vowed never to drink again until I was an adult.

When I arrived at school the next day, I walked towards my locker and noticed that the "Devastating Slims" had all been waiting for me with anticipation.

We'd met in the 6th grade and we all clicked! We were now four inseparable 7th graders. Stacey was tall, her slender build made her look "modelesque," she was quiet, but very matter-of-fact. Tarae was the shortest and had an attitude, so we called her Lil Bit', and Ferris was goofy and upbeat, she never had a down day and made us laugh all the time. We were junior high school cheerleaders, but we'd taken it a step further and formed a dance team called "The Devastating Slims," when we realized how much all of us loved to dance.

I picked up the pace because I knew this had to be good. When I approached the Devastating Slims, one by one they all gave their version of how handsome the new boy was. They announced that I'd just missed Timmy, the new boy, by only a few minutes. They were giggling and betting who was going to be his girlfriend. They were sure that I'd see him at some point during the day and we agreed to compare notes later at dance practice. Our town was so small that everyone knew each other and we always knew when a new kid moved in. An entire day went by, but I never saw Timmy, so I had nothing to report at our practice.

On my way home from practice I stopped by the arcade. Though it was a very popular spot for teenagers, Mama didn't like us girls hanging out there too much. I waited for my sister Wendy to get out of her last class, and we walked to the arcade as fast as we could to make the best of our time because my mother was known for tracking us down. When we arrived at the arcade there were several boys there already, and I knew all of them. I walked to the counter and ordered a pizza puff for Wendy and me to share. As I stood next to the counter I heard one of them whisper and then laugh, "Oh, they ain't doing nothing yet. Ms. Julie Mae don't play and she got a tight leash on them puppies." Another one yelled teasingly, "Hey, y'all." I looked at him, rolled my eyes and said, "Hey to yourself!" My sister and I giggled and remembered why we were there. We didn't have a lot of time because Mama would be home soon. I stepped around the "mannish" boys (or ill-mannered, as Mama would call them), and walked over to play Pac Man, my favorite game.

As soon as I approached the game, I immediately noticed that the boy already playing was someone I'd never seen before.

I got a clear view of him and my heart dropped. His eyes were big and brown and he was as chocolate as a Snickers bar. 'Oh my goodness, this must be Timmy.' It had to be. I knew all the boys from my 'hood and he was definitely not one of them. He noticed that I'd been staring at him and turned to face me with an innocent smile, "Oh, were you waiting to play?" I could not believe how deep his voice was and how grownup he sounded. My heart sank to my feet and I couldn't speak, I stood there for seconds without a good answer. I had no personality and was suddenly speechless. I had forgotten what he'd just asked me, but I nodded my head anyway, hoping the answer fit the question. It did. He smiled turned away and continued to play the game. I was still close enough to the door to run out and I knew if I took three steps backwards I'd be outside the door. I was perspiring and my heart pounded in unstable beats. I was experiencing puppy love and the embarrassment showed in my face; I needed someone to save me. He resembled an African prince, muscular with strong cheekbones and features.

There was no way I was standing behind him waiting for this game to be over! I walked backwards out of the corner and began looking for my sister. I spotted her and tilted my head toward the door, hoping she would understand the gesture.

"I ain't ready to go!" she yelled. She had just inserted her quarter into the Centipede game. I sighed and waited impatiently for her to finish. I knew it would be a while because she was really good at Centipede. "You can at least get our food!" she said. I hadn't noticed that our pizza puff was ready or that the cook had called the number written on the ticket he'd given me. I grabbed the food off the counter and fought my sister's annoyed glance. I couldn't stand to be in the same room with him, especially not after we'd shared stolen glances. I walked outside and decided I'd wait for my sister to come find me there.

"Why da hell you leave me in there? You like that boy don't you? He ugly anyway, but just ugly enough for you cause you ugly too," my sister said, laughing harder than I'd ever seen her laugh before. She knew how to push my buttons, but this time I laughed with her.

We skipped home and raced part of the way. She was really fast, but she couldn't beat me. I was an overachiever and reminded her that I was the big sister and she'd never win a race against me.

Mama hadn't made it home by the time we got there, so we got busy with homework and chores. That night I couldn't eat dinner. All I could do was think about Timmy. I couldn't believe how gorgeous he was. 'How in the heck did you fall in love after seeing a person for the first time?' The next day at school I waited for the girls to come to my locker. I couldn't wait to tell them that I'd seen Timmy. I hadn't really met him because I'd blown it and couldn't talk when he asked if I wanted to play the game, but I'd been in his presence nevertheless.

"Ooo, I hate you," Stacy said as she walked up to my locker laughing. She passed a note to me that had been neatly folded and shaped like an airplane. I opened the letter and realized right away that it was from Timmy. I wondered how he knew we were friends. I opened the letter and smiled as I read it. Timmy had drawn a large heart on the piece of paper. His handwriting resembled calligraphy -- the kind you see on wedding invitations.

Dear *De'Vonna,*
You are the most beautiful girl I have ever seen
Will you be my girlfriend?
Please circle **Yes** *Or* **No**

Not only did I want to mark yes, I wanted to write YES even bigger than he had it written on the note. There was no way I could be his girlfriend, my brothers and my mother would never approve. I'd already been told that I could not have a boyfriend. "I will let you know when you can have a boyfriend. Don't ask me, I will tell you," mama constantly reminded me. I reread the letter over and over again for the rest of the day. I didn't respond, but I never stopped thinking about Timmy and I getting married. We were *going* to get married. Yes we were, and my mother and brothers were not going to stop me. I saw Timmy at school during passing times. Each time, I giggled and dropped my head, ensuring that our eyes didn't connect.

Mama woke us up early the following Saturday and gave my sister and I strict instructions. We were to walk to my aunt's house to get flour. My aunt didn't live far, but I stomped all the way there because my brothers had bikes.

"Why couldn't they just go?" I asked my sister.

"Oh shut up. You get on my nerves. Let's just go get the flour and hurry back home. It's not far anyway."

My aunt lived a short distance from us so we arrived at her house in no time. I knocked on the door and couldn't believe who answered. I thought I was going to pass out. What was *he* doing at my aunt's house? This was crazy. "Here go your girlfriend Timmy," my sister said as she shot past me in hot pursuit of the sugar. Timmy and I both laughed, and when she was out of view he whispered, "How come you never responded to my letter?" It was as if my aunt knew there would be a connection between Timmy and I. Before I could answer his question, she walked into the room with squinted eyes, "What's going on in here? Don't y'all start that and have Julie Ann mad at me," she said as she chuckled loudly. Timmy was the nephew of my aunt's husband; it was truly a small world. I knew I wouldn't be able to visit my aunt as often as I would like once mama found out Timmy lived there. I stayed away from my aunt's house and was careful not to even mention his name around my house.

No one would know that I had a boyfriend. They couldn't know. I'd given him my home number and the specific times that he was to call. If my brothers answered he was to hang up. I was going to date Timmy no matter what anyone said. We had been talking on the phone one evening when my brother picked up the phone to make a call and overheard part of our conversation. He demanded to know who I was speaking to, so I told him, and he could barely wait for my mother to get home to give her the news.

"Ma, De'Vonna been on the phone talking to that boy Timmy that lives with Auntie B." My mother was livid! I had started my period a few months earlier, and she warned me that I'd better not be having sex. I cried that entire night, but I had made up my mind that they were not going to stop me from seeing Timmy. Timmy and I were not having sex. What we had was pure and special, and we were going to keep it that way. We continued writing and exchanging love notes and he sometimes wrote me fifteen-page letters and included songs from Freddie Jackson and Luther Vandross.
I read the lyrics over and over again and imagined Freddie Jackson serenading me at our wedding...

There's something that I want to say
But words sometimes get in the way
I just want to show
My feelings for you
There's nothing that I'd rather do
Than spend every moment with you
I guess you should know
I love you so
You are my lady
You're everything I need and more

The more I read the lyrics the more I loved Timmy. He started addressing me as "Sweetness" in all of his letters. We began holding hands in school and we each knew that this was the ultimate display of affection that sealed relationships in seventh grade. He carried my books and we had made it known that we were a couple. We had decided to seal our love with a kiss. Since mama didn't allow us outside when she wasn't home, I planned to have Timmy come to the back door so we could quickly kiss before anyone got home.

When Timmy knocked on the door my heart was beating fast. I couldn't imagine kissing a boy. We talked for a few minutes until I warmed up to the thought of kissing him.

We eventually worked our way past the formalities. "I don't bite," Timmy said, "and it will be a quick kiss. Just close your eyes." I closed my eyes and puckered my lips and he leaned in to kiss me, but as soon as our lips touched my older brother Bryce walked around the corner. "What the hell is going on!" he yelled. He grabbed Timmy's collar and pushed him against the brick wall that bordered our project unit.

"Man, I will kill yo' ass if I ever catch you kissing my sister again!" My brother looked at me with venom in his eyes. "Get yo' fass' ass in that house, and I'm telling Mama!" I did as I was told. I knew not to add insult to injury. Bryce thought he was our father and he would never go for me smarting off. My brother Eric walked around the corner just as Bryce was about to grab me and he dared Bryce to touch me, "Man, chill! Let mama handle it," he wouldn't allow Bryce to put his hands on me, but I knew I was in big trouble.

When Mama got home I got a good whipping and was instructed never to talk to "that boy" again. Timmy had been given similar instructions.

He'd been warned by his father and uncle to stay away from me. His father "didn't want any trouble" from my brothers.

I hated them all. They took away the one thing that I'd ever loved. Now I was going to be lonely again. I was heartbroken and couldn't eat for days. I was mad at everyone, but I couldn't talk to anyone about it. Timmy and I passed notes in school for a short time, and a few weeks later I heard that Timmy had moved on. He had started dating and having sex with a girl who lived across the street from me.

'How could he do that to me?' I was so hurt and enraged at everyone for breaking us up. It was their fault that he was now dating someone else. He never noticed the other girls until my brother threatened to kill him. I never told my family about Timmy and the other girl because I didn't want them to be proven right. "He only wants one thing," they said.

I moped around for months after the "breakup." When I didn't see Timmy around or at school anymore it made it easier to get over him, but I wondered where he was and what had happened. Then one day out of the blue, I received a letter in the mail from him. His dad had sent him back to Rockford to live with his mother. It was a pleasant surprise and I was happy to hear from him.

I'd heard from my aunt that when Timmy started to rebel his father stepped in. His father knew that Ford Heights wasn't the type of place where outsiders could come in and start trouble. He feared that his son would either get hurt or be killed. Timmy's father had made an important decision that may have saved his life.

I forgave Timmy and wrote him back. We kept in touch for over a year and promised each other we were still going to get married one day. We were going to have two children, and their names would be Timeesha and Timmy Junior. The thought of how black folks gave their children names to correlate with the father's name made me giggle. But, as the days passed I didn't think about him as often because life was taking many turns.

Mama came home from work one day wearing her scrubs. She had taken classes at the local community college and had gotten her GED and then entered a program to become a CNA (Certified Nursing Assistant). Although mama had been working as a CNA, she'd lost several jobs because she was not certified. In order to retain employment, mama needed her certification and she'd gotten it. Her days were longer now, but she was making an honest living, and many in the neighborhood finally respected the work she was doing. She grabbed the contents out of the mailbox and filed through the days mail while sorting the junk mail from bills. When she raised a thick letter in the air, I could tell it was not a form letter; this was something she'd been waiting on for a long time. Mama caressed the letter and held it close to her chest. It had come from the Cook County Housing Authority. She quickly ripped it open and began to read. Her grip was firm as if it was a piece of gold, she continued to silently read. My sisters and I sat at her feet in ignorance. Mama leaned back further into the couch and smiled as she closed her eyes.

"God, I thank you for your many blessings," mama said. The tears began to fall and she turned to us and said, "Y'all, we are moving out of the projects!" Mama had an excitement that I'd only seen from her on Christmas morning. We never expected toys because Mama had a way of hiding the gifts perfectly. While our friends had gifts piled to the ceiling, mama had found the perfect hiding spot. She only put gifts out on Christmas Eve, so the year we got Cabbage Patch dolls we were even more astonished than ever before. Back in the 1980s the Cabbage Patch phenomenon was crazy.

I remember the newscast showing people standing in long lines waiting for them, even fighting over a doll with a smashed face. Not only were there a limited amount of Cabbage Patch dolls sold at Christmas time, but they cost forty dollars per doll. That could put a damper in a single woman's budget, but my mother had bought four of them! We never questioned how she was able to afford the dolls; maybe she had saved up money from the card games she hosted. Mama knew how bad we wanted those dolls and we knew she had sacrificed something to get them for us. I remember tearing open the wrapping paper and jumping up and down on Christmas day screaming "We got cabbage patch dolls!" My mom sat and watched us as she wiped the tears from her eyes. That was the happiest I'd ever seen her, but this was a "different happy," and we were confused because we didn't know that Mama wanted to move. She had never complained about living in the projects. Who moves out of the projects, and why would we want to move? We had so many friends. We were sad to hear her say we were moving, but Mama wasn't sad at all.

There were mousetraps in every corner of our unit and we were catching two to three of them a week. The roaches seemed to enjoy the Raid and it no longer had an affect on them. No matter how clean a unit was, they were all interconnected and the mice and roaches went from one unit to another. If one unit was bombed by the Housing Authority it didn't matter because the roaches or rats always hung out until the "smoke cleared." We were still sad to leave. The projects had been our home and we had made many memories and friends. We were sad that we wouldn't be spending our last Christmas in the projects with the only friends that we'd ever known. Mama paid no attention to our sullen mood and continued to hum and sing as she mentally planned her escape.

"Y'all gon' get to celebrate this next Christmas in a house!" Mama said. We couldn't understand her joy at first, but the more she talked about how much space we'd have, the more excited we all got. Eight of us had shared three bedrooms for as long as I could remember. My older brothers would finally each have their own bedroom. I would still share a bedroom with my sister Wendy, but we wouldn't have to share with our two younger sisters.

Mama sent us to the store to ask Mr. Dejulio if he had any boxes he could give us because we had to start packing. We soon realized why Mama was so excited about the big thick letter. Mama had gotten her Section 8 voucher after being on the waiting list for eight years. Many single parents signed up for the rent subsidy because they wanted to get out of the projects and move into a house. It was common knowledge that it could take several years for an applicants name to reach the top of the list, but when it did it was worth it. People were paying little or no rent as compared to average rent costs. Mama was employed, so a substantial portion of her income still went to rent. Regardless of the cost, she weighed the benefits, and it was worth it to mama. We lived in public housing until I was almost fourteen years old.

Chapter 10

Closer to the Heat

The new house was still in Ford Heights, but it was out of the housing projects, where each year the violence had gotten worse. Gangs were now common, people were being beat down, and the drug situation had spiralled out of control.

We were now living closer to "The Circle" projects and my brothers had started to hang out with people that we'd only heard of before we moved into our new neighborhood. Our house was in "Golden Meadows," and there was an invisible barrier between the projects, Golden Meadows, and Sunny Field. Sunny Field was located on the eastern edge of Ford Heights and contained the largest majority of nuclear families, a mother, father, and children in the area.

Those homes consisted of working parents and their prestige was slightly above those living in Golden Meadows, but they were also, the working poor. Although Golden Meadows and Sunny Field were still in Ford Heights, it was considered better than being in the projects, at least in the minds of the families that lived in the houses.

Those children rarely played with the children that lived in the projects, and just like the other children who lived in Golden Meadows, we subconsciously *thought* we had upgraded.

We didn't realize that we were moving less than a half mile from the projects where we'd lived for most of our childhood. We moved into a blue three story house built in the late 1950s. It had a basement, a living room on the main level, and three of the four bedrooms were upstairs. Just as when we lived in the projects, we weren't allowed in the living room. The furniture had only been sat on by privileged adult guests, and everything was spotless and still looked new underneath the plastic protecting it.

Bryce's bedroom was in the basement. Mama liked having the finished basement because the boys were now out of her hair. They had become a little more lenient with me after the move. I think it was because they had started dating girls, and they didn't have time to keep tabs on me anymore. Besides, it was the summer before I was to start high school, and I was growing up.

I already had two aunts that lived in the projects, and my grandparents had just moved back to the Circle projects after living in a house for several years.

I wasn't sure why they had moved back, but I was happy that I'd always have an excuse to be there. Teenagers were always hanging out in the projects so I was looking forward to it.

The Circle and Golden Meadows had been separated by a large field of grass, but the children had walked through the field for so many years it had created a diagonal pathway. If there were any fights, the kids met in the pathway. In fact, most fights started and ended there unless someone dropped their books and took off running home.

My cousin Darlene lived in the Circle projects for most of her life. Everyone thought we were sisters because she looked more like my mother than I did. Darlene was a pretty girl and she wore blue eye shadow and red lipstick. We spent a lot of time together after we moved to Golden Meadows. I had even gotten mad at my mom once and ran away to her house. My mom found me hiding underneath a pile of clothes in Darlene's closet. Mama stormed into her house demanding to know where I was.

As soon as Darlene said "She is not here," her three year old niece walked over and pointed out the area of the closet I had been hiding in, "There she is Auntie," she said. My mother walked over to the pile of clothes and pulled them off of me and said, "Let's go." Darlene and I laughed about that for a long time.

One day as we walked through the pathway, Darlene saw David. "Here comes David's old butt." We both laughed and looked up as David closed in on us, he was a tall and handsome eighteen year old.

"What's up, cutie pie? You should call me some time," he said as he handed me his beeper number. Most of the teens, especially boys had beepers. Before there were cell phones, beepers were used to electronically transmit messages from one device to the other. I couldn't wait to make the call, but every girl knew you didn't beep a guy the same day you got his number. I'd seen David around town and thought he was cute, but he was older, and there were rumors that he had a girlfriend. When I asked him about his girlfriend he said, "Oh, she means nothing to me." David was eighteen years old, and I knew that would not fly in my mother's house.

My brother's friend Napoleon was at our house a few days later with a message from David. He whispered so my brothers didn't hear him, "David really likes you." I laughed, "Well, do you blame him?" He laughed without answering, and said that he'd make sure David and I got to know each other better.

"David's a good guy," he said. Napoleon agreed to be the liaison between David and me because he was dating David's cousin Sassy and saw him often.

If my brothers knew there was a love connection between David and I they wouldn't be happy. They would be even more pissed if they knew Napoleon was behind it all, so we all had to keep it very quiet. David and I passed messages between Napoleon for several weeks because we had to hide our newfound *friendship*. There was no way we could have maintained contact if it hadn't been for Napoleon. I was so thankful for him. Napoleon was a small-time drug dealer who made money selling marijuana. My brothers helped him bag "weed" in small baggies, so he was at our house a lot.

Now that my brothers were making money they were acquiring name brand clothes and there was no way they were making that kind of money on marijuana.

They had recently either purchased or been gifted with "Starter" jackets. When teen boys wore Starter jackets it usually meant they were dealing drugs. Parents in the projects were poor and had larger families, and most of them couldn't afford to buy Starter jackets. My mother definitely couldn't afford them.

We got new clothes every holiday, but mostly on an as needed basis; when school started, Easter, the Fourth of July, and at Christmas. There were special occasions in between when mama sacrificed and bought new clothes, such as the time that I'd placed in the district spelling bee! Mama was so excited and wanted to make sure I looked good when I stood on stage. She went to Kmart and bought me a pair of Rustler jeans with a red and white checkered shirt, and to Payless to buy me brand new penny loafers. I searched all over the house for a worthy penny to grace the slot in my loafers! I felt good that night as I accepted my third place trophy in the spelling bee, but mama made me feel as if I'd come in first place. Regardless of the occasion, name brand clothes were always out of the question in our household. So, it was obvious that my brothers had moved up the chain doing *other* things to access quick money.

I knew it because I'd walked into the basement one evening and saw the white substance on the coffee table. There were piles of powder and piles of a hardened, tan-colored substance. I shrieked, "Oooh, Mama would kill y'all if she knew what you were doing down here!" When I found out what they had been up to Bryce threatened me, but his voice was losing the power it once had. "Get upstairs before I get mad," he said. I barely moved when he spoke to me these days and I took my own sweet time walking up the stairs. There were times when I'd peak downstairs to see what they were doing and I'd catch sight of the piles on the mirror. I wondered if they were testing the supply.

Chapter 11

The Big Set Up

But, until unmasked, I would describe him as nothing but myrrh, and balm, and ringlet, and diamond, and flute-like voice, with pleasant and mirthful conversation

-Author Unknown

Napoleon stopped by one evening while my brothers weren't home. He was at our house so often that it wasn't unusual for him to be there even if they weren't. I wasn't shocked to see him, but I asked anyway, "what are you doin' here?" He had a silly expression on his face and didn't answer right away. I gave him a quick, sharp look and asked again playfully, this time demanding an answer, "What the hell you doing here?" I was suddenly suspicious of his intentions because something seemed a bit off with him. He looked nervous, "I know I've been trying to set you up with David, but I can't imagine you dating him. I really like you and if I didn't have a girlfriend you would be mine." he said.

I was floored by his admission, but I had to admit that I'd been feeling the same way. It made me nervous to hear him say these things, and he sounded nervous when they escaped his mouth. He was my brothers' friend and something didn't feel right about that.

I noticed that in the last few weeks our conversations would begin with references of David, but ranged from several different topics, such as school, friends, sports, and local gossip. I hadn't said anything, but I'd gotten used to talking to him every day for hours at a time. Everyone liked Napoleon. Even more, everyone liked talking to him - girls, guys, men, women, the young and the old. He had the kind of personality that would make anyone comfortable. We spent a lot of time on the phone that summer and he dropped by on hot summer nights and sat on the porch to keep me company. He was someone that I'd gotten to know very well, and I had fallen in love with him without realizing it. There was something in his voice that activated the butterflies in my stomach. He had become my new best friend, and I hadn't realized that he was the only person I talked to on a daily basis.

Napoleon had spent almost an entire summer hiding his feelings for me and pretending that he wanted to set me up with David. No wonder David and I hadn't gotten anywhere. Napoleon was blocking it! "Oh my God, You have been cock blocking all summer!" I said, laughing uncontrollably. "You're right," he said, "I have, but it's been hard because David is really into you."

His face slowly turned serious as he placed both his hands around my waist and kissed me on my lips. He whispered in my ear, "You are so beautiful, so special...and so different," and though it had been a quick kiss my body silently responded. I was embarrassed by what was happening and reminded him that my mother may be home soon so he'd better be going. He agreed, but said that we should keep this quiet because people might get the wrong idea. On his way out he reminded me that we could not tell anyone because David and Sassy would not understand. He grabbed my face between his hands and kissed my forehead. I closed the door behind him and rested my back against the door as I slid to the floor deep in thought.

When I finally rose from the floor I floated upstairs to my bedroom and sat up in my bed reminiscing about Napoleon. I replayed the scene in my head hoping to seal it into my long term memory bank. I wouldn't forget this night. *Ever.* I closed my eyes, fell back onto the bed and stared at the ceiling engrossed deeply in my thoughts.

'Wow, he kissed me, there were no interruptions, and it felt good.' My heart skipped a beat. Nothing about making out with him felt wrong. In fact, it had felt perfect, and that night in my dreams, we made love.

A few days later Napoleon called and asked to speak to my brother.

"Is Eric home?"

"Nope, he's not here -- is that the only reason you called?"

"Of course not, when can I see you again?"

"Whenever you want, just open the front door!"

"You are not outside silly!" I said.

I quickly ran down the stairs and opened the door. There he stood with a huge cell phone up to his ear; it was still very awkward to witness people holding gigantic telephones up to their ear.

I laughed and told him he looked silly. "You know you want to make a phone call," he said sarcastically.

Before I closed the door, I nervously looked around to make sure no one saw him come inside. As soon as the door closed behind him he grabbed me, kissed me, and held me tight. I'd never been held like that before, and I felt like a woman. "I can't stop thinking about you," he said as his voice shivered. It felt right to have his arms around me. He pressed his lips against mine and caressed my hair. He led me to the couch and fell on top of me, one leg after the other. Suddenly, I was afraid. My heart felt as if it was going to jump out of my chest. If my brothers or my mother walked in and saw us gyrating on the couch we would both be dead! He sensed my fear and assured me that they would not be home anytime soon.

"Don't worry, they're not coming."

"How do you know?"

"Trust me, they aren't coming."

"I'm scared Napoleon."

"Don't be afraid, I love you. I am here for you, do you trust me?"

"Yes, Napoleon...I trust you."

I was under his spell, and didn't feel fass. I was freely giving myself to someone that I cared about. He was going to make love to me and I wasn't fighting it. I wanted it, and I needed it. I had never had the freedom to say no. People had come into my bedroom and touched my body and penetrated me in ways that I was too young to understand. My body had been subject to experimentation time after time without being old enough to consent. I had been a victim, but tonight my mind was made up and I had freely said yes. Napoleon had entered my private place and I was perfectly okay with it. With every stroke, I was being purified from every impure thing and the penetration was cleansing to my soul. No more would someone come into my bedroom and touch my breasts. No more, would someone touch me in places I had not given them permission to touch me. I was releasing the hurt of my past and all the disappointments that I'd ever experienced. As he made love to me I promised myself that I would never remember the things that had happened to me before him. It was a done deal, my mind was made up and I would love him forever. I'd freely given him my soul and he had become my savior. Napoleon could not begin to conceive the power that I'd given him that night. That night was about much more than sex. It was a renewing of my entire being. I'd been cleansed from all that had come before him, and the depth of what had happened that night could not be understood by a mere boy. That moment was a breakthrough for me. The things that took place that night eradicated segments of my past that grieved me and I would be released from them forever.

That night, I lost my virginity.

Chapter 12

He Loves Me

Oh, Napoleon...Napoleon! I belonged to Napoleon. Thoughts of him made me smile and I couldn't wait to hear his voice again. When he showed up at my house the next day riding a moped I was ecstatic.

"So, you gon' ride me?" I asked. He looked at me and smiled.

"C'mon, get on. That's why I'm here!"

"Wait, I need to go change."

I was wearing my track shorts and gym shirt from Cottage Grove Middle School. He smiled.

"Hey, don't worry, you have great legs and you look good in anything."

I looked down and smiled, I had to agree with him, my caramel-colored legs didn't have a scar on them. I'd run track all through junior high and the strength of my muscles showed in my legs. I ran my hand down the side of my well defined legs, "I guess you're right." I giggled and jumped on the back of the moped.

Girls were outside jumping Double Dutch, boys were playing basketball in the park, and adults were standing around talking and "shooting the breeze." It felt so good to be leaning up against his back as he rode me around town, I was on top of the world. As we yelled to each other through the blowing wind, the words were lost in the breeze, but we didn't seem to care. All that mattered was that we were together at that moment. I didn't want the ride to end. We rode around for a couple of hours, and had been through all but one of the projects, the one where Sassy lived. It didn't matter because I knew people would spread the word about me being *straddled* on the back of Napoleon's bike. Good gossip spread like wildfire in Ford Heights. Big Daddy always said that "an idle mind was the devil's workshop." I'd always been told that once a boy gets what he wants he doesn't come back. But after we had sex he never missed a day of coming to see me and he made me promise that I wouldn't have sex with anyone else. Napoleon pulled up in front of my house, and I reluctantly got off the bike. I didn't have a hair out of place because I'd just gotten finger waves.

He gave me fifty dollars that day and said I should spend it however I liked. Fifty dollars for ME! I was fourteen years old, and that was a lot of money! I got off the moped and went into the house. The phone rang just as I kissed Napoleon goodbye, and I could hear it ringing repeatedly as I entered the door. I answered with a lingering smile on my face and a hand on my hip.

"Hellooooo," I said, still out of breath from running to catch the phone call. "Little girl, I know you don't call yourself liking Napoleon?" I didn't respond, so she repeated herself. "De'Vonna, I know you don't call yourself liking Napoleon." It was Sassy, Napoleon's girlfriend. Sassy was eighteen years old and Napoleon was her boyfriend, so I definitely could not admit to her that Napoleon and I were involved. I braced myself for the story I knew would soon come. I had already been scripted by Napoleon.

"If Sassy ever asks you if we are messing around or if I've ever tried to have sex with you, tell her no," so I was ready. "Oh no," I responded, "We're just friends." She responded with a tone filled with a sharpness that I didn't hear from girls my age. "Oh, okay because I don't have time to be kicking no little girl's ass."

Her voice trailed with highs and lows that I'd only heard from adults and her tone suggested that she was in charge and I was to listen and wait until she was finished speaking. She was angry and wanted me to know that I better stay far away from Napoleon. "Ummm hmmmm," she said. I stood in my kitchen holding the phone in disbelief, and before I could say anything else, Sassy had slammed the phone down in my ear.

I hung up the phone a bit shaken and immediately paged Napoleon to tell him what had happened. "Don't worry about her, I got it covered. I love you, and I'm only with her because of the baby." Sassy had given birth to their daughter the summer before. I'd already had anxiety about what would happen if I crossed Sassy's path. I definitely wasn't ready to see her and I was still trying to keep it a secret when David called to ask me if the rumors were true. Sassy told him that she'd heard about me having sex with Napoleon. 'How did a ride on a moped translate to stories of me having sex with Napoleon?' "Yes." I told David, "I'd taken a ride on Napoleon's moped," but I adamantly denied having sex with Napoleon.

In fact, it seemed that I'd spent the entire summer denying the rumor. 'How did everyone find out that I'd been having sex with Napoleon?' I hadn't told anyone but my friend Stacey and I doubted she was spreading it. People were asking me if Napoleon had "popped my cherry." When I asked Napoleon if he was telling everyone that we'd had sex, he denied it and of course I believed him. He said he would "never do such a thing." I was getting sick and tired of hiding my relationship with Napoleon, and it wasn't fair to David. Napoleon pleaded for me to never stop seeing him. "I love you and I've never loved anyone but you and Sassy, please don't shut me out of your life," he begged. I didn't want to stop seeing him, but this secret relationship was tearing my heart to pieces. I had become weak to his tactics, my mouth was saying one thing, but my heart was saying another. My soul was tied to Napoleon. I tried many times that summer to end the relationship with him, but I was deeply in love. Every single time I told him that it was over he whimpered back to my house and begged me to give him one more chance. I was preoccupied with Napoleon, and though it wasn't fair to David, he had simply become an alibi.

Regardless of how much I tried to break it off I couldn't seem to move forward. David and I dated for a year, but I never stopped loving or spending private time with Napoleon. No one understood why I loved him so, and neither did I. Eventually, David moved on and our relationship had finally come to its inevitable end.

My early years of high school were a blur because I was too busy focusing on Napoleon and all that the relationship entailed. I didn't pay much attention in school and managed to pass ninth grade with a C average. As long as I was passing, I could fly under the radar, so I only focused on passing. I floated through ninth grade and passed on to tenth by sheer luck.

The pregnancy rate had skyrocketed at my high school and the administration added an entire wing for teen moms. Girls that I had attended junior high school with were getting pregnant. The district had taken immediate action to decrease the amount of pregnant high school dropouts by creating an on-site daycare, making it easier for young moms to attain their high school diploma.

I didn't want to be a teen mom, so I made a mental note to stop by the clinic one day on my way home from school to get birth control. I couldn't believe Napoleon and I had been having unprotected sex for over a year. Eventually pregnancy was my least worry because Napoleon had a new agenda; he had started seeing other girls, and neither Sassy nor I could stop him.

I was becoming a woman and enjoyed meeting and hanging out with new people. During my sophomore year I became friends with an older girl named Paula. Paula had a body that made heads turn and whenever I heard the Commodores' song "Brick House," I thought of her. She had hips that black men loved and her body was envied by most women in the projects. Paula had a great personality; she was funny and her quick wit always made her the life of every party. She was worldly and knew a lot about life. I looked up to Paula because she was so wise. I'd seen her around town and admired her demeanor, she was mature and classy. Paula understood street dynamics, and how things operated in the projects.

It was widely known in Ford Heights that "Paula's slick ass," could get money out of a rock." She was a hustler and a master at winning things, especially when it had to do with telephone redial. The radio station WGCI conducted a birthday game every week, and the fifth caller whose birthday fell on the announced date could be the winner of a thousand dollars. Paula knew how to rig birth certificates, so it was most important that she got through the line. That had never been an issue for Paula and she had already been a winner many times, so what she really needed was a *recipient*. Paula won the money and gave me the winnings, and I used it as a down payment on my first car. My brother co-signed for me because I wasn't old enough to purchase a vehicle.

Paula and her son lived in The Vietnam housing projects. I couldn't wait for the weekend to hang out at her apartment because Napoleon and I hooked up there every weekend.

Sassy had been telling people that when she saw me, she was going to "kick my ass." I wasn't worried about running into her anymore; I'd cross that bridge when I got to it. I'd gotten to the point that I didn't care anymore.

I couldn't get enough of him and he couldn't get enough of me.

Napoleon had become a celebrity of sorts in our town. He was dealing drugs on a much larger scale than before and had lost old friends and gained new ones. My brothers didn't hang out with him anymore, they said "his head had gotten too big and he had changed." The last few times I'd seen Napoleon I'd noticed a change in his attitude too; he'd become cocky and overly self-confident. He was moving on to bigger and better things.

Chapter 13

Chain of Command

Drug dealing had become a career for many in Ford Heights and young boys aspired to be the *next* big dealer after dropping out of high school. They believed this goal was more attainable than other career options. When drug dealers drove new cars, wore nice clothes and had lots of money, they caught the attention of many, including young girls. Napoleon had control of the Circle Projects, but Lucas, Kojac, and Big Boo were in charge and ran a separate drug operation on Fifteenth Street.

Big Boo was big and black. He grew up in the apartment right behind ours and I'd known him all of my life, just as I'd known the others. Lucas was an unassuming, quiet, lovable, family man. He was an average size man with boyish features, and had married his high school sweetheart. Kojac was different from the rest. I couldn't imagine him being in charge of anything, controlling a group of hoodlums? I couldn't see it, but he did it with ease and pizzazz.

Lucas's crew initiated the drug game on Fifteenth Street. They were once enemies of Napoleon's, but only for a short time; they'd collectively come to a truce and figured out that they could each make money because they were on separate sides of Ford Heights. Most thought they'd come to a truce because neither of them were real warriors. If they had been, there would have been turf wars and someone would have either gotten hurt or killed and that would have been the end of it.

There were other petty drug dealers in Ford Heights, but Lucas and Napoleon made progress that had never been achieved in the drug game. By purchasing small samples of crack cocaine with their girlfriends' welfare checks and flipping the profits they were able to gain leverage. Drugs were purchased with small amounts of money and then sold to make a profit. When that profit margin was achieved, the drug dealers went back to the supplier and made larger purchases. In some cases the dealers reached such a pinnacle that they were selling large amounts of drugs to petty dealers and establishing themselves as suppliers.

Lucas, Big L, Big Boo, and Napoleon had reached this point, but their success had also established each of them as moving targets. Life had become dangerous. Big L was Lucas's boss in the drug game. I assumed he'd gotten started the same way the others had. Big L had not grown up in Ford Heights with the rest of us, but he fit right in because he was down to earth, wise, and soft spoken. He had taken a liking to my brother Bryce and took him under his wing; he introduced Bryce the drug game.

Mama had suspicions that Bryce was dealing drugs, but she couldn't prove it. He had started providing for himself and helping us around the house and giving mama money to help with the bills. My mother was adamant about her feelings toward drug dealers and she constantly reminded my brothers that she "did not raise them to be drug dealers and if she ever found drugs in her house she would turn them in to the police." They knew mama was serious; she did not want "dirty money" in her house.

Lucas and Big L stopped by our house to pick Bryce up quite often, so we got to know them both very well.

They treated me as if I was their little sister and would often slip me a few bills to go shopping or to get my hair done.

Many of the teen girls were wearing expensive gold jewelry, herring bone necklaces, diamond cut rings, and gold link chains. Some were either dating older men or petty drug dealers, and all the money was being spent on hair, clothes, shoes, jewelry, and other materialistic items. Big L gifted me with my first gold ring and I knew sooner or later I would add to the collection, it was inevitable.

The drug game had caused extreme tension between the small time drug dealers and the big bosses in Ford Heights, and there had been rumors that someone had put a hit out on Big L. We never believed it would actually happen, so on the day he was killed we were all devastated. He'd become a part of the family. Big L had been standing on the corner talking to friends when a fifteen-year-old boy we all knew walked up behind him and shot his brains out. The drug game had taken one of our beloved friends and his children would be raised without a father.

After Big L's murder, Bryce had an epiphany and walked away from his big dreams of becoming a reputed drug dealer. But, his death didn't stop the drug sales in Ford Heights, and production only ceased for a couple of days after the murder because every one knew the police would be "hot on the scene." As everyone assumed, not long after Big L's death, Big Boo and Lucas immediately took over production and became the new drug bosses of Fifteenth Street.

Lucas and I remained good friends. If I ever needed money all I had to do was call him, I could count on him for anything and he knew he could count on me. Lucas and I conducted countless business transactions, and I was his decoy. I had accompanied him to undisclosed locations to drop of several packages. If the police saw a man and a woman riding down the highway, they assumed the *nice* couple was going on vacation. What they didn't know was that the trunk was filled to capacity with large plastic bundles of powdered cocaine. It would soon be delivered to another state and converted to crack.

Drug bosses didn't trust many people; they couldn't because the odds weren't always in their favor, it could be detrimental.

Life wasn't easy and carefree as it had been for Lucas before he started selling drugs; now he had to think about his every move. We greeted each other with a kiss and a hug, it was a sure sign that we loved each other, but we never crossed the line. I was like one of the boys and he knew he could trust me as much as he trusted Big Boo and Big L. I'd known and loved him long before he was a well known drug dealer. He'd taught me most of what I needed to know about the streets, preparing me for what was to come. "Don't get caught up D, you better than this." I took his advice to heart, and hadn't planned on getting caught up.

I understood how Lucas and Big Boo had expanded their drug business. Big L had moved from Chicago and showed them how it was done, but it was shocking to find that Napoleon had been so successful in this ruthless drug game. Napoleon controlled several blocks of drug territory in Ford Heights, and if someone tried to take make money on his turf, the "The Crew" either asked them to leave nicely or imposed a brutal beating on them.

"The Crew" was comprised of people from the town we all knew; boys that had grown up right in Ford Heights who were now drug dealers. Crack cocaine was creating great profits for the drug dealers and even bigger losses for the families in Ford Heights that were affected by its plague.

I wanted to witness what Napoleon was up to. I'd only heard about the dealings, but I had to see for myself, so I asked Paula to walk with me to the Circle projects where his enterprise was located. We agreed to wait until the sun went down to take our walk. The hottest part of the spot was right across from the unit where Napoleon and Sassy lived. As we approached the housing projects, we saw brake lights for at least two blocks. Paula gasped, "What the hell is this, rush hour?!" Traffic was bumper to bumper on the residential street! People were pulling up to buy drugs and Napoleon's staff were exchanging crack for ten dollar bills, the transactions were taking place right out in the open. It was unreal. 'Where was the police', I wondered? One of the staff members spotted Paula and I, and it made him visibly nervous.

He walked towards me quickly stuttering, "De'Vonna, what are you doing over here? Does Napoleon know you are down here?" His tone was almost a whisper. I looked at him, laughed, and then responded, "He doesn't need to know where the hell I'm at," and I pushed my way past him. By the time we made it to the next block, we noticed that we were being followed by a black, shiny Cadillac, it pulled up next to us and the tinted window rolled down. It was Napoleon.

"What are you doing over here?" he asked sharply. I looked at him and rolled my eyes. He really felt that he controlled my every move, and was shocked that I'd walked through his enterprise and interrupted his flow. He did not want Sassy to know that I was walking around on their turf. No. That would not be good for him. "Get in the car, De'Vonna," he said. I didn't move, I was enjoying my walk. "There's nothing wrong with taking a *nice* little walk, this is a free country Napoleon, and you ain't my daddy!" I snapped back with a smirk. I hadn't seen him in almost a month. I was so happy to see him. He smiled back. "Get yo' hot ass back where you belong.

I'm going to have Sammie bring you some money so you can go shopping in the morning." He knew I'd respond to that. I sighed. "Okay, Mr. Napoleon. I'mma call you 'Mister' from now on because I see you over here doing big things. I'll see you later." I winked at him, smiled, and put my hand on my hip. "Come on, Paula girl, if we hang around this area too long we might end up strung out on crack, too." Then I looked back at Napoleon, "Oh, by the way, we gone walk, but thanks for the offer." Paula and I giggled uncontrollably. I slowly walked away from the car and turned around. Paula and I were dressed alike in skinny jeans, tank tops, and color coordinated jelly shoes. Napoleon slowly scanned my body from top to bottom as his eyes made their way back up again. He dropped his eyes at about waist level and blew a kiss. I smiled, and knew what that meant. I'd see him later. We continued on our walk and noticed that his workers were busy directing traffic. The police rode by and waved at everyone without asking any questions about the crazy traffic jams.

There were rumors that Napoleon had the police on his payroll. It had to be true because he was making lots of money, and no one was going to jail. He had ascended from being a petty drug dealer to a baby kingpin. His operation seemed to flow smoothly with three shifts of workers on his payroll. He'd bought every one in his clique cell phones, when most adults were still oblivious to how these contraptions worked. Napoleon was running a very sophisticated system from the housing projects, making more money than working people, and he was a high school drop out!

We walked back to Paula's house and waited for Sammie to drop the money off. "I bet that gay bastard Napoleon bring that money himself," Paula said. "He is strung out over you, girl. He don't love Sassy. She just knows all of his secrets, and she can have him locked up. If he had a chance, he would be with you." I didn't spend too much time trying to figure that one out. For the time being what we had was enough for me.

"You are too pretty and smart for him. Move on with your life, you are not second class," everyone told me. It was what we shared that made me feel special. Napoleon and I were friends.

Spending time with him was like hanging with one of my girls. When we'd talk, I'd get so caught up in the conversation that at times, I'd blurt out, "Girl...you wont believe what happened next," then we'd both realized what I said and burst into laughter.

Of course, I was overly excited when Napoleon knocked on Paula's door and brought the money himself. I'd had a hard time connecting with him lately and it really bothered me. His *new* life required that he trust no one. I wrapped my arms around his neck and hugged him tight; the gun he carried inside his breast pocket poked me. I didn't acknowledge that I had felt it; I wanted him to feel safe.

"I know I haven't been by in a while, but I have to lay low right now," he said. Napoleon had been robbed at gunpoint by masked men and he was now paranoid about every move he made. Paula lived deep in the projects, across from a large field of grass where searches had turned up dead bodies. Visiting me was now of grave concern to him and he'd expressed it on more than one occasion, "Why are you always over here and not at your mother's house?" he asked. His comings and goings were now being detailed by people who wanted to rob him, he was not himself.

Napoleon seemed extremely distracted as he paced back and forth across the room. He was no longer carefree because now he had things that everyone in Ford Heights had always wanted – money and power. People knew that he was making a lot of money, and he was now a target for hustlers, robbers, and women. His life had changed and he had to "watch his money" because the workers were now "stealing and hiding money and drugs."

I was growing up and my mind was starting to expand and venture. I had dreams of being someone special, dreams of making something out of myself. I didn't want to be a project girl who aged out on welfare. I'd seen where that could get you. Oh no, I was going to finish high school and maybe go to secretarial school or something and get a certificate. Big dreams. I had big dreams.

Chapter 14

Testing the Waters

Things were changing quickly in Ford Heights. It wasn't uncommon to hear the sound of bullets ricocheting in the midday sun, so we had become accustomed to hearing and dodging bullets. Not only were people poor in Ford Heights, but crack cocaine had emerged at an alarming rate; this added to a desperate situation, causing people, and the town to literally deteriorate right in front of our eyes. Some parents were experimenting with crack, and eventually we were starting to notice that they had quickly transformed from respected parents to shameful addicts. We were seeing crack cocaine's hold as it physically transformed adults we'd known all of our lives to zombies whose status and respect had been reduced to shaky leeches with eyes that no longer focused and hearts that seemingly no longer cared.

My cousin Darlene and I were walking down the street and a known gang member ran past us bleeding from his head and mouth.

Immediately, a group of his fellow gang members passed us in hot pursuit. We were stunned because we'd known him to be a tough boy, but it had become evident that the gang life could break any "tough boy" down. Later that day we heard that he'd gotten a "violation" from the gang because he had broken one of the rules and the Vice Lords had made him pay.

All around me teens were drinking and using drugs, and girls were getting pregnant at young ages. Many kids my age were doing drugs and usually it started with the gateway drug, marijuana, but I had recently moved beyond "weed." We had figured out how to take weed smoking to another level. In addition to purchasing a bag of weed, the new thing was to purchase a small bag of crack cocaine and add it to a joint. It wasn't hard to get crack because it was being sold on every corner. I'd become a professional joint roller, and could roll one with my eyes closed. After perfectly covering the rolling paper with marijuana, I would sprinkle crack cocaine across the joint to prolong the high, this duo was called a "primo."

A primo couldn't be rolled too tight or too loose because it affected the way it burned, and we didn't believe in messing up a good high. Smoking a joint and adding a "lil something to it" was more acceptable than smoking crack from a pipe. We weren't "crack heads."

I remember the morning that I realized a crack addiction had set in. I'd gotten up wanting and needing to inhale a primo. But, I felt an intense barrier between what I wanted and what could be a detriment to my life. It was no secret that crack was lethal, but I never believed I would become addicted. My body craved the mix of drugs that it had grown accustomed to. I hadn't brushed my teeth or eaten breakfast, but I needed to make a phone call to get the drugs that I desired. As I walked toward the phone something happened, and it stopped me dead in my tracks. I felt my spirit connecting to something greater than me and I knew it was God. An intense revelation was occurring and I heard it loud and clear. "You are chosen. Hear the voice of the Lord." It was as if Elder Hutton stood right there in front of me speaking. It frightened me to feel, hear, and acknowledge the revelation.

I wasn't going to church anymore, and I definitely didn't consider myself a "Christian," but I knew that I'd clearly heard the voice of God. Suddenly, I knew it was over. I was not going to ever *smoke* crack again. I stood in front of the phone frozen in my thoughts analyzing the months leading up to today. I'd spent many hours smoking primos and being preoccupied with maintaining a drug habit. In an instant, I was overcome by feelings of guilt and remorse and the desire for the deadly mix of drugs had instantly disappeared. That was the last day I smoked a primo, but it would not be the last time I'd do drugs. The revelation wasn't enough to tame my wayward spirit, and by the end of my sophomore year in high school I'd been through so many highs and lows with Napoleon that I'd started to accept that we would never be a couple.

One night I found myself in The Velvet nightclub strictly out of boredom. I went to sit down and heard a familiar voice calling me, "Come here niece." She beckoned for me to follow her into the ladies bathroom.

Without a second thought, I followed her. I'd known her all of my life. Malory was really not my aunt, but many people claimed to be related in Ford Heights. She was once a pretty woman; I'd seen old yearbooks that showcased her beauty and vitality.

She wasn't the young, pretty, healthy-looking woman that she once was. She'd spent many nights in the bar drinking and getting high, and it had taken a toll on her. She paraded around the bar with lots of energy, but I knew that ten to fifteen years from now she'd either be dead or very close to it if she didn't change her lifestyle. I followed her into the bathroom, and she pulled out a piece of folded white paper filled with powdered cocaine.

"This is for you," she said smiling. I laughed and said, "Auntie, I don't do that stuff. Do you have some weed?" She smiled at me and responded, "Listen niece, after you sniff this you won't want any weed." I justified my desire to try the powdered substance, 'Folks didn't get looked down on for sniffing cocaine.' I had vowed never to *smoke* crack again.

Everyone subconsciously believed that smoking crack was more addictive than "tooting" it, but it was those very misconceptions and justifications that caused many to be strung out on drugs long before they realized they were addicted.

In a split second, I decided that there was no one in the bathroom but us. No one would ever know.

I could just sniff it and move on with life. I nodded my head and she unfolded the white paper even more. I slowly slipped my pinky finger down into the powdery substance duplicating what I'd seen in movies. There was enough of it inside the tip of my fingernail to test. I looked at the delicate powder as I gently pulled the substance closer to my nostril, being real careful not to spill any. I moved my finger closer to my nose, slowly and strategically. Then, with one quick whiff, I inhaled the precious cocaine and sniffed every particle resting inside the tip of my fingernail. The substance burned my nose as it found its way into my system. I held my head back in ecstasy and remembered my troubles no more.

"Mmmmm, I liked that Auntie, let me try it again. I gleefully prepared my pinky for another dip.

I left the club that night in complete euphoria. I didn't have a problem in the world and I wondered when I'd see *Auntie* again. I walked out of the Velvet and debated if I would walk to Mama's or Paula's. I flipped a coin in my head. I'd go to Paula's, she was closer. As I began my walk I made an assessment, my high was wearing off. I stopped on the sidewalk to stare into the night sky, it was magnificently clear and I was mesmerized by the beauty of the stars. 'God had numbered every star' and tonight I could count each of them if I wanted to. I couldn't believe how calm the night was, the perfect summer breeze was invigorating.

I snapped out of my stupor when I heard the excess vibration screaming from the pipes. It was extremely loud but intoxicating. My love for motorcycles heightened my senses, but the bike's hum was close, closer than I'd originally estimated. 'Was it Gavin?' I wondered. I hadn't looked back. We weren't involved but I knew there was a mutual attraction. Would he recognize me and just ride past? I smiled without turning around and stood still with my hands on my hips and rested in a hard pose, I still hadn't looked back. Now, I could feel the warmth of the pipes on the back of my legs.

Its owner had maneuvered onto the side walk where I stood. Slowly, I turned to face him, and my excitement suddenly dropped, I was disappointed. I hoped it was Gavin; instead, it was *him* - Rashad. He was a constant fixture in Ford Heights, but lived in Chicago Heights.

I'd heard that Rashad had the deputy chief of detectives on his payroll and the word on the streets was that detectives were keeping him out of prison in exchange for ten thousand dollars a month. I dismissed the thought.

This man was not made of spare parts. He stood in front of me; his frame over six feet tall, and his face that of Grecian descent. He was beautiful. Is this how the Greek God Apollo had looked? It was certainly how he'd been depicted in story books; attractive and strong. Rashad was a black belt, trained by his father, a master karate instructor. His father had successfully competed in Karate tournaments in the United States and Canada. Rashad had been trained by the best. As he glared into my eyes, a boyish grin slowly came into view. He had the power to captivate. And, like Gavin and Shane, both drug lords in their respective cities, Rashad had made it big in the drug business.

He was the right hand man to Shane Dominick and was in charge of a drug empire that they successfully built together. He was what the little boys aspired to be. He was their hero, but how did he become friends with Shane Dominick? They were two different personalities. Rashad's smile was devilishly beautiful, his eyes dangerously mystical, his reputation, ruthless.

It was true that I'd never seen him fight or stir up trouble, but his kind didn't do those kinds of jobs on their own, at least not in public. There were many in his entourage willing and ready to be at his beck and call to do the unthinkable. They were willing to suffer any consequence for the almighty Rashad. His infamous tales of torture were due to drug deals gone bad. The things he was rumored to have done behind closed doors made people steer clear of him. His long legs hung from his frame as his feet fell to the platform. 'How could someone so beautiful be so dangerous,' I wondered.

"Whattup D?"

"Nuttin Rashad."

"What you doin out so late all alone."

"Nuttin, just felt like getting out."

"Must be really bad for you to be out alone, I've never seen you by yourself, you know you run with a pack."

"Well, everybody need some time alone. I guess that's how it goes sometimes."

"You want a ride home?"

"No, I don't have a long walk, I can make it," I said.

I was coming down from a cocaine high and still rationalizing the risks. I didn't want people to assume I was sleeping with him. What if Napoleon saw me on his bike? More than anything, I didn't want Rashad to get the wrong idea. Though I declined the ride, we continued to talk. Cars whizzed by and periodically someone I knew would wave from their window and yell my name. I debated whether I should go back inside and find auntie because my high was nearing its end. I decided against it.

"Well, I better be going Rashad, it was nice talking to you, guess you aint so bad after all," I said with a dry laugh.

"Come on, I can take you home, it's no big deal, jump on."

Without any further thought I hopped on the back of his bike. We floated off the sidewalk and onto the highway. I held on tight as he accelerated and switched gears. Rashad yelled through the warm breeze, "Do you like motorcycles?"

"I love motorcycles!" I yelled back. My hair blew in the wind. The speed of his bike was thrilling. Napoleon's moped couldn't compare to this. I was like a kid in a candy store.

"Hey, I live down on Park Lane. "I know," he responded. As we sped down Lincoln Highway, he passed the street leading to my house. "I want you to see how fast this thing really goes." We floated down the highway and intersected onto a major highway. I wasn't afraid. I leaned into him as the speed of the bike accelerated.

"Slow down," I said.

"No reason to be scared," he yelled through the wind. As he slowed down and exited from the highway I loosened my grip.

"Where are we going?"

"I have a quick stop to make."

When he pulled into the hotel parking lot, I pushed the nervous thoughts out of my mind. He shut the ignition off.

"I'll just wait out here," I said.

"It may be a few minutes, come in, I won't bite. I promise."

I took a deep breath and inhaled thick oxygen, I clenched my fists and reluctantly exhaled. I didn't want to be caught coming out of a hotel with Rashad, this was not my plan.

I knew I had no desire to be with him and I didn't want to go in. I had two options. I could sit outside the hotel on the bike and look silly or I could disappear when he went inside. But, where would I go? This man was probably harmless. 'I was overacting,' I told myself...there was no reason to be afraid. I inhaled again, and this time the oxygen was thicker. I was afraid.

'This would only take a second.' I exhaled.

"Okay, okay" I said.

The doors to the hotel rooms were outside, so we didn't have to enter through the lobby. He got off the bike and I followed him inside.

"It will only be a minute," he assured me. "I have business to take care of, just gotta get this little thing finished and then I will take you home."

"Okay," I sighed.

He walked ahead of me with confidence and control, but there was more in his stride. His presence was intimidating. As we entered the hotel room, he motioned for me to have a seat in the chair. I scanned the room and noticed that the desk was completely clear other than the Chicago Tribune that hadn't been touched.

No sign of real work being done there. The room encapsulated the bare necessities; a bed, a closet, a bathroom, a desk, and a chair. What *work* could he have been referring to? 'Did he live here?' There were freshly pressed dress pants and jeans covered in plastic hanging in the closet. I picked up the newspaper and started to read. A few minutes later Rashad walked out of the bedroom wearing his underwear. My heart dropped. He walked up to me as I sat in the chair and grabbed the news paper out of my hand. I lowered my chin toward the floor.

"Look, this is not why I'm here - you were supposed to take me home."

"I will take you home, but I have some business to take care of first."

"Rashad," I paused. I didn't come here for that. You said you were going to take me home!"

"Listen here bitch, you are going to fuck me and you are going to fuck me now." There was no where to go, no witnesses. No out.

"I don't want to do this."

"Yeah, that's what you say now."

'Was he serious? Who was this person? He was not the man I'd talked to in front of The Velvet. How many women had he done this to?' His eyes had grown dark. Possessed by something evil, he grabbed me by my neck as I struggled to get away. With one hand he pulled me from the chair and forced me onto the bed. I fought to get away but he was too strong.

"Don't fight it."

"Don't do this Rashad."

"You know you want me."

"I don't. Please, just take me home!"

"Naww baby, I can't do that right now, I have wanted you for too long." My fears had been confirmed and I was about to be violated again. I gasped for air as I tried to escape the tightness of his grip. My heart beat faster and I could almost feel the blood's path trailing too quickly to designated destinations.

'Was the intensity initiated by a final rush from the cocaine I'd ingested?' His hands were tight around my neck as the hot tears slid down my face. I lay beneath him scanning the room and being forced deeper into an unknown place. The room began to spin and I could no longer focus. My breathing was now occurring in slow, weakened gasps.

"Stop…Rashad…stop." I begged between gulps of air.

"Don't cry now you little bitch, you walk around here like yo shit don't stank, like you're all *that*." He was strong and I couldn't fight him, if he killed me no one would know. His hands tightened around my neck. It was my fault; I should have never gotten on the bike with him. Finally I was escaping his grip, slowly losing consciousness. My eyes rolled in the back of my head and I couldn't breathe. My thoughts were suffocated and I was trailing off into any unknown place. He held on to my neck. My head pounded. I didn't feel well. 'Lord help me.' I utilized each free breath to speak in an almost inaudible whisper.

"Stop, I don't want this," I pleaded between shallow breaths. He held one hand on my neck as he tugged at my pants. I was too weak to fight him off; fighting against his power was useless so I gave up…

Fear and shame overtook me as I lay there with my eyes closed for what seemed like an eternity. I'd heard the water running from the shower in the bathroom, but didn't want to believe that I was still there with him. I was afraid of his reaction but I couldn't share this space with him any longer.

I opened my eyes and the darkness slowly dissipated. It was then that I realized I had passed out. The room was dim, but I heard birds chirping. It was morning. I blinked to focus on my surroundings and I remembered exactly where I was and how I had gotten there. I was lying on a bed wearing only my shirt and my bra. My pants and my panties were missing. I didn't remember him penetrating me, but I knew it had happened. The realization of the night before hit me like a ton of bricks when I heard him speak.

"Get up and put your clothes on." My head was pounding, and the headache was almost unbearable. I felt like crap. I stumbled to get out of the bed. When I didn't respond he repeated himself. "Get up and get your clothes on." He was still naked when he walked past the bed without looking at me. I sat on the edge of the bed in a daze. I watched him get dressed and was disgusted with what I saw. Rashad was a rapist. This would not have happened if I hadn't hopped on that bike. He walked to the window and opened the curtains.

"It's a beautiful day out there, huh? Nice day for a ride," he said, as he turned around and smiled at me. I didn't speak. I couldn't respond. I thought about what he'd said in front of the Velvet, "I don't bite, I promise."

'Was this normal?' I'd paid a high price to see through his armor. He nonchalantly handed me my panties and my pants and asked if I wanted to shower. When I declined, he picked up the key to his bike. "Let's go," he said. I quickly got dressed and followed him down the stairs without speaking. As I watched him climb on to the bike I was numb, and didn't move fast enough for him.

"C'mon, get on," he said. I did as I was told.

"I don't wanna hear anything about no damn rape either, he said. "You wanted it."

I was sure this was the same authority he used with his boys in the hood or with any other girl who went for a *ride* with him. He wanted me to know that he was in control. This line came too easy. He'd said it before. His method of luring me here was second nature. I knew he had done this before, I was not the first person that he had raped and I knew there would be many other young girls. No one would have the courage to report what Rashad had done to them, not even me. His threat was useless. I hadn't planned on ever telling anyone what had happened. Rashad had been given power by those around him. Many young boys and men looked up to him, and girls were at his every whim.

Somehow this power equated to getting whatever he wanted no matter the cost. No was not an option, even if it meant rape.

As we rode off my body detested any contact with him. I leaned forward, numb. As he accelerated, the wind forced me to press into him. I didn't care if I slid off the bike. My hands and then my body slumped even deeper into him. I was sliding off the bike, slowly dying inside, no longer caring if I lived or not.

"Dammit hold on before you fall off!" He yelled. I did want to fall off. I wanted to slip off the earth, fall off and land in traffic; that would deaden the pain.

At least the pain of getting hit by a car would have been swift! The sun was shining, but I didn't acknowledge it.

When Rashad stopped in front of my house, I slowly got off the bike, still numb, and now, not caring if anyone saw me. I was vexed, a walking zombie consumed with shame. He turned to me and smiled. "Here," he said, as he extended his hand to pass me his business card. "Let me know when you want to get together again." I did not respond. I was in shock. Did he not understand the magnitude of what he'd done? I slowly extended my hand to receive it. I turned away and walked toward my house. I'd never call him. Ever.

Then it hit me! *It* was happening, *again* -- the roaches, them nasty stinkin' roaches. Still multiplying! I had to forget about them. Tomorrow would be a new day.

Chapter 15

Love's Inception

I would never tell anyone that Rashad had raped me. I had moved on. I would get through life without ever having to talk about it, but I continued to blame God for all of the things that had happened. How could God allow me to go through what I'd gone through? Where had my father been? If I'd had a father he could have protected me. I'd hidden things in my heart that I hadn't told a soul, yet, I continued through life as if I was *normal*. I began to tell myself that life was a dream, and if it was a dream then I'd wake up from it one day and wipe the sweat from my brow. Other times I'd tell myself that life was a movie set and I was the director. Whenever I was ready to say "cut," it would be over, and I could clean the slate and start all over again and make things fresh and new. That was how I coped with the things that had happened.

I dreamed most nights. Sometimes I'd remember them, and other times I wouldn't.

It was always interesting to lie down at night because I never knew what I'd dream about. Often I'd wake up and share my dreams with Paula. One morning I slipped into her bed and nudged her awake. I tried to whisper, but I was too excited!

"Guess what Paula? Girl, I dreamed that I was getting married. I wore a beautiful white wedding gown and the wedding was held in a huge church, and everyone was there; friends, family, and people that I didn't even know! They were all happy for me." Paula rolled over, laughed, and said, "Girl, you are drunk. Get yo' drunk ass out my room." I slapped her leg hard and joined in her laughter. I rolled off the bed onto the floor and pushed myself up from all fours as I walked out of her room.

I was in a very serene mood because I'd never really thought I'd get married until that moment. 'Me? A wife?' I didn't even know many people that were legally married, other than my grandparents. There were some, but not many. Most men and women we knew, lived together as common law couples for decades, even though Illinois didn't recognize common law marriages.

Tonight, I felt that it was possible. I'd tasted the cake in my dream, and I'd never experienced a dream that seemed so real. God knew that I would have to taste the cake in my sleep; otherwise I wouldn't have believed it. 'Oh my God, I'm getting married!' You would have thought I'd been asked and the ring was already on my finger! Maybe Napoleon would finally break up with Sassy and marry me. Then again, maybe I'd marry David and finally grow to love him. Now that was a funny thought. I'd only wanted to marry Napoleon. But, I was beginning to feel that his hold on me was starting to loosen, and I think he knew it. Things were coming around full circle, and these days Napoleon seemed to be wondering where I was. I was moving on to bigger and better things. Life had started to pick up at a fast pace and I had gotten a fake ID and had been partying in adult night clubs on a regular basis.

Chapter 16

Manifestations of Silk

It didn't matter to us that we were all packed like sardines because the adrenaline was flowing. Chantilly Lace perfume permeated the air as we curled our hair, put on makeup, talked, laughed, and drank Boone's Farm while getting dressed. It had taken us nearly three hours to get dressed. Paula, Fran, Tisha, and I were all taking turns in the bathroom at Paula's tiny apartment. Fran had put her son to bed before the sitter arrived and joined us.

Aaliyah had finally arrived full of energy, she walked quickly to where the children were sleeping in the living room to look in on them. She was a skinny girl, but a cute kid, and very mature for her age. She had to grow up fast because her mother was on drugs and she was the caregiver to her five sisters and brothers. Aaliyah loved spending time with us. Normally we didn't let young girls hang around us, but she was ahead of her time. She'd say things that were quite profound for a girl her age from the projects.

"What if there is a life outside Ford Heights?" Her question was one worth pondering, but I never imagined leaving Ford Heights, so it didn't really pertain to me. This thirteen-year-old was a master at conversations, and though I enjoyed listening to her, I had to get dressed! I ran back up the stairs to perfect my make-up.

"Heyyyyy now!" We all chimed in unison. We could hear the bass from the music banging as we walked towards the Silk Carpet night club. We were still blocks away, but our excitement was heightened at the sound of music flowing out of the lounge. When we finally approached the door of the Silk Carpet Lounge, the DJ was playing our song. Johnny Kemp's version of "Just Got Paid" was blasting through the speakers!

"Come on y'all, I'm gonna need a fire hydrant!" I screamed and laughed as we headed through the door. The lounge was usually filled with people from Chicago Heights and Ford Heights, and they would be dressed to kill. The Silk Carpet was a bit classier than the Red Velvet, but the similar set up made this place a deathtrap too, one way in and no real exit.

The place could hold 150 people, if that. There were cars parked bumper to bumper at every corner surrounding the building. It was packed beyond capacity. Just how we liked it. We'd partied at the Silk Carpet every Friday and Saturday night since I'd gotten my fake ID and according to my ID card, I was twenty-one years old. If there was ever a bust, I'd be covered and so would the club owners.

It was our practice to make a dramatic entrance. Our haters would be waiting, and we didn't want to disappoint them. There was smoke everywhere, and eyes cut our way, both men and women. I'd worn a teal, sleeveless, form fitting body suit. I was a woman now, and I wanted everyone to know it. Everything had fallen into its rightful place and was well proportioned. Gosh, did seventeen look good on me. No longer angry that my breasts had outgrown me; I thanked God for blessing me with them after I turned fifteen. Back in the sixth grade every girl in my class had breasts but me. I'd been teased for putting tissue in my bra. Two of the older girls in my class had walked up to me and squeezed my wad of tissue. Then, one of them declared, "Your titty is crooked," and tried to change its form to look more natural.

For the next six months I started a ritual of doing chest raises and chants, "I must! I must! I must increase my bust!" I'd read the rhyme in a teen novel and believed it worked. But today it was obvious that God had done a good job, and I was hoping that both those girls were there to witness the goodness of the Lord. I frantically dug deep in my purse for the fake ID, while attempting to remain calm.

When I crossed the threshold with my girls in tow, the juvenile laughter stopped, and I put on my best you-better-watch-out-I'm-here look. My entrance was obvious to a particular someone. He was standing at the front door and had informed the doorman not to charge us a cover. He winked at me, and I winked back as I sashayed towards the back of the club. I knew it was going to be a good night.

Gavin was one of the owners of the lounge and had been flirting with me for at least a year. "Drop that loser and get with a real man," he'd said. "He ain't letting Sassy go anyway." If he hadn't been ten years older, I probably wouldn't have given it a second thought.

He was strong-minded, cocky and opinionated, and didn't care who didn't like it. He was a drug dealer-turned-entrepreneur and had lots of money that he loved spending and showing off. That, of course was a turn on for a little girl like me from the projects. People respected Gavin, not for being a ruthless drug dealer, but they loved him because he loved Ford Heights. Gavin continued to fund events for families in need long after he had gotten out of the drug business.

The place had begun to fill up and there was no longer walking room. Wherever you were standing was where you were stuck unless you ended up on the dance floor. In most cases I always did. I moved through the sea of people and looked around to see who I could spot in the crowd. As I pushed my way through, I immediately noticed someone trying to get my attention. She was waving wildly and running towards me. I admired everything about her. She didn't know how gorgeous she really was or how many women would die to have her high cheek bones, her perfectly curved figure, smooth chocolate skin or her pretty white teeth. She stood 5'7 and was all legs.

It was my sister Wendy. We looked nothing alike; in fact we were total opposites. Her body mirrored Grace Jones, strong and tight, but her facial features were soft and beautiful. She could definitely pass for a model. Her zest for life was contagious. As the deep brown chocolate beauty ran towards me, I realized that she was really running past me to the dance floor. As if it was an after-thought, she remembered what she'd wanted to tell me. She looked back towards me and yelled, "Oh, Girl, Napoleon just pulled up, he's outside waiting for you." I hadn't made plans with Napoleon! And, I certainly wasn't about to leave my girlfriends to go hang out with him. Things had changed and it had become obvious to every one but Napoleon, that his spell had been broken. I no longer jumped at his every command and these days he was pursuing me more than ever. I rolled my eyes and ran to the dance floor as I heard the club anthem. *Atomic Dog* piped through the speakers strategically positioned throughout the building. The floors vibrated in tune with the bass as we moved our hips to Parliament's popular tune. No one was in control, the drum beat had taken over and we methodically snapped our fingers, threw our hands in the air, and rolled our hips. There was no way I was going to miss this song, "Tell him I'm on the dance floor," I yelled back, as I ran to an open spot on the floor. Minutes later I looked over and my sister had attracted a large crowd around her. She never made it outside to report to Napoleon. I laughed. She danced like no one else in either of the two cities, and everyone loved to watch her.

There was an exuberant energy coming from the dance floor and it summoned everyone to join in. People swarmed to the dance floor, hips were swaying, and hands were in the air. Every inch of the dance floor was occupied. I had run to the dance floor with my long island iced tea in my hand and my purse still on my arm. With precision I dropped my derriere about four inches from the floor and arched my back to the beat. I was in rare form and this was the only song that could take me there. The bass was pounding through the speakers, and my sister's audience loved the show she was putting on. It took the attention off me, and I could just dance to the beat however I pleased with no one watching. It seemed this song would never end, and I didn't want it to. When it did, my sister and I high-fived each other and agreed that no one in the club could dance like us.

We laughed, but I knew she was the real dancer. They teased that I "danced like a white girl." Maybe it was true to some degree, but my rhythm was precise. There was no beat that I couldn't find. I loved music; it had taken me places where nothing else could. I swayed to the bass lines and jumped on the saxophone chords until the beat lessened to degrees that were inaudible. I didn't care what they said. When I was on the dance floor, I was in a place no man could take me.

I strolled off the dance floor to Gavin's attention. He'd been watching me the entire time. He walked over to me just as the next song began to play and grabbed my hand as he pulled me towards the dance floor. "Come dance with me?" I wondered if he'd requested the song. By then I was sweaty and hesitant about dancing another round, but how could I say no? He was dressed to kill wearing leather pants and a Coogi sweater that looked great on him. Only a real man could get away with wearing leather pants. I imagined Napoleon in leather pants and laughed out loud.

I had never even seen Gavin dance with anyone at the club before. Now he was coming to grab ME to dance to Keith Sweat's "Right and a Wrong Way to Love Somebody." I couldn't believe it. I was nervous as he held me. The lyrics were beating in my chest as they played through the speakers...

You may be young, but you're readyyyy.
Ready to learn.
You're not a little girl.
You're womannnn.
Take my hand...

I could barely move, I knew by morning Napoleon would know that I had danced with Gavin, and he would not be happy about that. The more I thought about what Napoleon would think; I realized that maybe he needed to hear something about me for a change. I loosened up and began to enjoy the song. Gavin pulled me closer to him as his hands slowly shifted to the small of my back. His hands were now dangerously close to my rear end and I felt my heart beating fast. I was attracted to this man. Gavin was built like a weight lifter, solid and precise.

He held me tight, and I didn't want him to let me go. When the song ended we hugged and I walked off the dance floor, careful to look straight ahead. I didn't want to see the accusatory glances from anyone in the club.

Just as I was about to take my seat, I noticed an astounding beauty headed my way. All eyes were on her as she made her way to the back of the club where Gavin and I had just danced. Her perfect asymmetrical bob hair cut was precise and not a hair was out of place. She'd been very shy and quiet in high school, but her beauty alone had caused her many enemies. It was my cousin Zarita. She wore a striped cotton baggy pant suit. I focused in on her and noticed her oversized blouse hanging strategically off her shoulder with a belt around her waist. We were both seventeen, but this girl looked twenty five, she was gorgeous! She made heads turn. She walked over to me and gently smiled, "I saw that! You is sooooo fass," she said. We both laughed as I led her to the table where the others were sitting. Zarita was not like us, in fact, she was different from any of the girls in the club. She had attended *Holy Ghost Deliverance Center* all of her life, and hadn't been exposed to many of the things that we had.

She had been raised in a religious home with two parents and had been shielded from the things that we project kids were subjected to. Her confidence could easily be pegged as arrogance. She was a Bentley, and she'd been taught early on that she was royalty; it was just evident that she believed it. Zarita's father and my mother were first cousins and our grandfathers were brothers. I thought back to the first time we'd really hung out. I remembered being at her parent's house and her father explaining why she couldn't wear pants. She stood toe to toe with her father wearing a long denim skirt and a t-shirt. Her skirt hung past her ankles, as she stood fearlessly next to her father while he spoke, "The bible says that a woman should not wear anything pertaining to a man." Her father was adamant. His voice was gentle, and he didn't yell as he expressed his beliefs. I'd worn pants all my life and so had all the girls in my neighborhood. Her parents had invested a lot of time into her and had taught her the principles of holiness, but she was growing up, and when girls grew up they tested the waters.

Parents could not stop what was inevitable and regardless of her father's beliefs, her parents had loosened the grip and there she stood…in pants, and beautiful as ever! I cleared my throat as my hand trailed down the front of my neck making sure she heard and saw me, "Don't you see I'm thirsty, buy me a drank girl." I knew how to make her laugh. Zarita dug into her purse and pulled out a huge wad of cash. "Damn, you selling drugs? Where did you get all that money?" I asked, laughing. She slapped me on my back and said, "Same place you get yours from, my man!" Zarita still bore an innocence of someone new on the scene; she was quiet, soft spoken and didn't use profanity.

We stood at the bar waiting for our drinks and a handsome suitor about fifteen years her senior walked over and stood between us. He slipped one hand around her waist, and said, "Oh, so this is your cousin De'Vonna? I've heard a lot about you." I gave Zarita an accusing look, "It better been good." He was about six feet three, clean shaven, and looked like the business men that I'd only seen on television. His crisp dress shirt and perfectly creased black pants hung perfectly across the top of his shiny shoes.

My cousin and I looked at each other and smiled and I could tell that she was really digging him. I hadn't seen him in person, but she'd told me all about him. Shane Dominick, the kingpin of Chicago Heights. Napoleon and Lucas were not in his league, he was the ultimate big fish, the catch that every girl in the hood had hoped for. Zarita had gotten him. They looked at each other and he signaled that it was indeed time to go. Zarita and I shot each other knowing smiles, and then, from across the room, I saw him. Wearing all black, Shane had waved coolly at the gentleman looking over at us. I couldn't make out his face, but I would never forget his aura. I wanted to run when I saw Rashad, but I froze in place as he approached us. As he closed in on us, I wondered what he'd told Shane. It didn't matter; I knew I needed to move! I needed to get out of his path. 'Had he seen me?' 'Did he know who I was?' He searched for my glance as I turned away from his smile. I forced my brain waves to connect with my thoughts - 'run!' Making sure not to appear suspicious, I quickly hugged Zarita and strategically moved through the crowd.

Rashad was never again to be trusted. I turned to make sure he wasn't following me and I saw the back of his head as he exited the club. He was a rapist and I would never allow him in my space again.

I found my way back to the rear of the club and Paula and I danced the night away. When we left the club that night our hair was soaking wet from sweat. Gavin offered to take me and all the girls out to breakfast, but both Wendy and Fran had dispersed by then, they each had steady "booty calls." Paula and I waited for Gavin to count his earnings from the evening. When he was finished, we headed to the only joint still open at four-thirty in the morning. Paula had given her approval, "Get that money, girl!" And so it began. My relationship with Gavin started with a phone call, and escalated quickly to dinner, chats, long drives around the city of Chicago, and ultimately a love connection. I'd been eating at places I'd never heard of. I'd never really been outside of Ford Heights other than doctor appointments.

We had a laundry mat, convenience stores, and a library. Everything we needed was right in Ford Heights. Some would say "that's how the *man* wanted it," for us to continue to be separated from civilization and for things to remain the way they had been for many years.

I was at Gavin's house so much that he'd given me a key, but I couldn't use it unless I'd confirmed it with him first. One morning Gavin went into his dresser drawer and pulled out a pager and gave it to me. "I need to be able to get in touch with you, and you better call me right away whenever I page you." He'd bought me a beautiful gold ring with a pearl as the center stone. Gavin thought it was tasteless for a young lady to wear rings on every finger, and in his presence, I scaled back.

I cut off all communication with Napoleon, but, when I saw him in public, my heart skipped a beat. My mind and body was done with Napoleon, but my heart hadn't gotten the message yet. I pushed thoughts of him in the back of my mind, and finally life was moving forward without my first love.

Gavin had started supporting me financially and I didn't want or need anything. I was shopping on a regular basis and didn't have a job. I'd just turned eighteen and we had been having a full-fledged relationship for almost a year. I'd casually moved back into my mother's house and she hadn't asked any questions. She was just happy to see me around the house again.

I'd left my old wardrobe at Paula's and replenished my closet at Mama's with all the new things that Gavin had bought for me. Mama had come home from work one day and looked through my closet and questioned where I was getting money to buy all the things I had. She asked me to join her in the living room so we could talk. I knew this wouldn't be good.

"I know I haven't always been there for you. I've been busy working and taking care of seven children on my own. I have done the best that I know how. I'm a single parent, and I do the best I can for all of yall. I'm not on drugs, I have been a good mother, haven't I? This aint neva been a *hoe house*...I have not brought men in this house around yall." Mama paused and held her head down, she was fighting her tears.

She raised her head up again and continued, "I've been hearing rumors that you are involved with Lee. You have more clothes, jewelry, and shoes than I do. Hell, you have clothes in there with price tags still on them! I know you are sleeping with some grown man. Don't make the same mistakes I made De'Vonna. You have so many more opportunities than I had. Don't mess up your life like I did." I'd never seen my mother so distraught.

She was grieving the daughter she knew she was losing to the streets. I could feel my mother's pain, but there was no way I was going to confess! Besides, the rumors weren't true. I wasn't sleeping with Lee, I was sleeping with Gavin, so it wasn't a total lie when I responded, "Mama, I'm not sleeping with Lee." Lee was Gavin's close friend and business partner. Where Mama had gotten her information from, I'd never know, but I knew it wasn't unusual for people to get rumors mixed up in Ford Heights.

The freedom that I'd attained since I started seeing Gavin allowed me an escape from everything and everyone. I wasn't about to lose that now, not for Mama or anyone else.

Chapter 17

Invincible Love

There had been a knock on the door while I was in the shower, and Gavin yelled for me to stay in the bathroom until he got rid of whoever it was. I tiptoed out of the bathroom and could hear a female's voice. I could not believe he had allowed another woman in the house while I was there. I was upset, jealous, and enraged.

'What if he'd been telling her he loved her too? Was she my competition? Was she the reason we had to hide our love for each other? What if he's showering her with gifts and having sex with her too?' Before I could rationalize my thoughts, I stormed out of the bedroom wearing nothing but a towel. I pranced out of the bedroom and into the hallway and made eye contact with an older version of myself. Gavin stood at the bottom of the stairs in disbelief. My wet hair dripped down the back of my neck as I stood at the top of the staircase.

I pressed my arms against my breast to create the illusion of a perfect cleavage. I posed in the most seductive stance I could think of and stood there and smiled. She must have been at least twenty years old. She was beautiful, with big brown eyes, a fair complexion, and light brown hair. I looked directly into her eyes wanting her to know my thoughts, 'I'm here with him, I have the power and I'm the one he's chosen.' She looked at me in disbelief and then she turned towards Gavin. "I hate you!" she spewed at him as tears filled her eyes. She turned towards the door and ran out of the house devastated. I was wearing an internal smirk and I was very proud of myself for being so assertive, but Gavin was not happy with me. He looked at me and said, "That was really lowdown of you, I cannot believe you did that D. After all I've done for you? Get dressed, you need to go!" I felt vindicated by my actions, but I allowed him to finish venting. His voice was stern, but he didn't yell. He was very matter-of-fact with his words and was not accepting my apologies or justifications.

I had made the ultimate mistake by revealing our relationship to one of his lovers and he had declared that our relationship was over.

I'd been calling Gavin for over two weeks and he would not return my calls. He was adamant about needing "some time." I couldn't believe he was actually going to just cut me off. 'What was he thinking?' I tried to explain to him that I really cared about him and I was only jealous when I realized that he'd been seeing other women. I guess I'd always known it and had accepted it, but the reality of it was painful. Even after I had shown up at his house unannounced to try and win him back, Gavin wasn't hearing it.

"You need to move on with your life, we are done." I couldn't believe he was dumping me. The temporary fix was over and healing had come in the form of a bandage named Gavin and material possessions, and now that he wasn't there anymore, I had to face the music. I'd been able to mask everything that I'd been through, and Gavin was ultimately a distraction from my inner battles.

Chapter 18

Inevitable Change

I grieved the breakup with Gavin for a couple of months when I received a letter in the mail from Timmy. 'My first crush, Timmy. Oh my God,' I was so excited! He invited me to come to a birthday party that his family had planned for him. I'd already decided that Paula would come with me. That morning I got up, washed my hair, showered, and pulled myself together. Paula would be so happy. She'd been consoling me for weeks and didn't have any faith that I'd get over Gavin anytime soon. I pulled up in front of her house in my Chrysler Lebaron. Paula answered the door wearing a long satin gown; I stood on the tip of my toes and looked over her shoulder, suddenly suspicious of who was in her bedroom. She sensed my suspicion and laughed, "Girl, stay out of my business, let's talk about you," she said. I laughed and ignored her comment. "Girl, the drought is over. Jesus done revived me, and we are going to Rockford next weekend.

Timmy invited us to his birthday party!" She was ecstatic, but wanted to know where we would be sleeping while we were in Rockford. I assured her that our lodging should be the least of our worries, and it would all work out. Without taking a breath, Paula said, "Girl, we have to pack, we have to go shopping, and for sure we have to get our hair done. I'm so ready to leave this dump! A vacation is just what we need." We spent the rest of the week finalizing travel plans.

Now that I wasn't dating Napoleon or Gavin I didn't have any extra money, so I turned to my old tricks, the trusty five finger discount. That meant all the free clothes we wanted if we could make it out of a shopping mall without getting caught. It was so easy to do back then. We'd take a shopping bag with us, go into the store, remove the price tags, fill the bag up, and walk out. Paula did not want my sister Wendy to go to the mall with us that day, and I didn't blame her. Paula reminded me of the only time that we had ever gotten caught shoplifting. My sister had been the one to get caught, but she turned toward us and said, "Come on, De'Vonna and Paula, they caught us." We all knew that *we* weren't caught. *She* was caught, but we had all been arrested.

We were juveniles so our parents were called and we were immediately released, but we had vowed to never take Wendy with us again. Even though Paula was apprehensive about letting Wendy go with us, she agreed, and we got away with more clothes than ever.

By the time we left for Rockford my sister had decided to join us. My mother would not be happy about that. She was only seventeen years old.

"Mama is going to kill me if I take you," I tried to talk her out of it, but she wasn't taking no for an answer. "If you don't take me I'm telling Mama where you are, and you know that won't go over well with her." I finally gave in. "Okay, we'll tell Mama that we're staying over Paula's this weekend." I was too excited about my getaway to debate with my sister. Besides, Timmy had once again come into my life at a time when I needed him most and it had to be God. I wasn't going to make this trip a debacle by fighting with my sister about it. Hell, we'd all just go and have a great weekend. I smiled to myself and continued working out the preliminary details in my head. I decided that I was going to get over Gavin sooner than I expected.

From the first mention of the trip to the actual departure, we had managed to include both my sister and Fran. The drive to Rockford took us about two hours and we had fun on the way down. I'd been the designated driver since it was my car. We sang, talked, laughed, and flashed truck drivers. The closer we got to Rockford, the more ecstatic we got.

When we pulled up at Timmy's mom's house we were all in shock. From the outside, the house looked like an unkempt farmhouse. There were at least three stray dogs walking around and they looked malnourished as they walked around the mass of junk in the yard. The grass had died from a lack of both water and sun. There were several cars in the driveway, and most of them didn't seem to be operable. I could feel Paula glaring at me from the passenger seat. She had created visions of grandeur in her mind and this was surely not what she'd imagined. "What the hell is this?" she asked. I shared her sentiments, but didn't verbalize my thoughts, at least not at the moment. I agreed with Paula, but I tried not to show any emotion. I hunched my shoulders and raised my eyebrows without opening my mouth to answer.

"It'll be fine, it's only a weekend. We'll go to the party and head out on Sunday night." Wendy let out a steady, hearty laugh. "Paula, you live in the projects. You can't look down on anyone!" she blurted. Although Paula lived in the projects this was definitely the boondocks and we were afraid of what we might see when we went inside.

We were reluctant to get out of the car because the stray dogs were coming. When we finally exited, one of the dogs licked Wendy's ankle. She kicked at the dog trying to shoo it away. "Look here mutt, keep your nasty tongue off me! You probably been eating maggots all day long!"

"Oh leave those dogs alone, they didn't ask to be here." I was always the one to look on the bright side of things, but I was glad the dogs weren't licking me. I knocked on the door and a woman answered, wearing a house gown, a scarf on her head, and a cigarette in her mouth.

"Who y'all here to see?" she asked with a roughness in her voice. We explained that we were there to visit Timmy and that we were from Ford Heights. "Oh, okay, come in. He'll be here shortly.

He been expecting y'all," she said. Without showing any enthusiasm, she introduced herself as Mary, Timmy's mother. I'd heard a lot about her over the years, but this was my first time actually meeting her. She had dark circles around her eyes and I wondered what she'd been through in her life, if she'd been abused as a child, or if she'd ever had any dreams or aspirations. All I knew was that she didn't smile much, and more importantly, she didn't seem very happy to see us. The girls sat on the couch and didn't say much. I tried to initiate conversations with Mary, but they fell flat. She never engaged me and I tried not to take it personal.

When Timmy arrived three hours later we were happy to see him. We'd been sitting at his mother's house on the couch waiting for him and were in desperate need of a meal and showers. He walked in with a smile on his face, but there was something different about him and I couldn't put my finger on it. We were definitely not the same kids who had met in the seventh grade.

Timmy quickly informed us that we would be staying at his older brother's house. On our way to his brother's house we realized that Rockford was similar to Ford Heights, there were drug dealers on almost every corner and the poverty was undeniable. It appeared that the crack phenomenon had either started here first or its addiction had set in at an alarming rate. Just like Ford Heights, there were equal numbers of churches and liquor stores on every corner.

When we arrived at Capone's, he wasn't home. Timmy introduced us to his live in girlfriend, Barbara. She was twenty-seven years old with four children. She was very nice and we were grateful for the warm reception. We all thanked Barbara for allowing us to stay at her house, and we were shown our sleeping quarters - Paula, Fran, and Wendy would share a bedroom, and I would share a room with Timmy. We got settled and took a nap to rest up for the evening's festivities.

Not sure how long I had been sleeping, but I was startled to find Timmy staring at me when I woke up. "What a weirdo you are," I said before rolling over and turning away from him.

He smiled and said, "De'Vonna, you don't even *know* how beautiful you are. You are so pure and there's an innocence about you that is so calming.

You are everything I've ever wanted in a girlfriend. I'm so lucky to have you." I smiled back, but my innocence had been taken away many years ago and I'd accepted that there was nothing *pure* or *clean* about me. I was damaged goods, so it made me sad to hear Timmy refer to me as this "spotless" being. He thought I was perfect and it made me cringe. I sat up, thanked him and slid out of the bed. I quickly got dressed and headed downstairs to see what the girls were doing. I was both surprised and envious to find that they had been awake and were already conversing on the couch. They were too excited and couldn't sleep. Barbara had made fried chicken, macaroni, and green beans and they were now eating, but I noticed a very familiar look in Paula's eyes, I'd seen it before. 'Oh no,' she had met Capone! Now, she was foaming at the mouth. I sat on the arm of the couch next to her and chastised her with my eyes, "Stay away from him," I signaled. She leaned over as close to my ear as she could, without knocking me off the edge of the couch.

"I'm in lovvvvvvve," she whispered. I reprimanded her, "There is NO way in hell you are going to screw around with Capone. You are going to get us all killed!" Capone walked in the room, came over to me, and gave me a hug. "Hey...I finally get to meet the infamous De'Vonna! I've been hearing about you for too long. Welcome to the family sister-in-law, it's nice to finally meet you. Boy, my brother knows how to pick em," I laughed, but my humor was short lived. Capone looked Timmy straight in his eye, with a voice of an authoritarian, "Man, don't mess this one up. You got a treasure on your hands."

I attempted to provide him with my most humble thank you, but something about the intensity in his voice had gotten my attention. This was much more than brotherly advice, I shook it off and reminded myself that it was only a weekend and whatever Timmy had going on it wouldn't be my problem.

I understood why Paula was attracted to Capone, he was handsome. His complexion was dark and smooth, his nails well manicured, and he dressed well. When he walked into the room, he commanded your attention and his presence was undeniable.

I secretly wished Timmy was more like his brother, but I knew in my heart that he'd never be the man Capone was.

Paula stood up from the couch and planted one foot in front of the other. Her silhouette was perfect as she slid one hand down her hip. She looked me straight in the eye as she released the weight to her other hip, demanding the attention of everyone in the room. She bent down and whispered in my ear, discreetly placing her derriere in Capone's direction. I had to give it to her, she had a "banging" body and no words could describe the way her hips were attached to her frame. She was well aware that she held the attention of everyone in the room. She was accustomed to causing a stir and I knew she liked the flurry of secret glances. "Look here, Missy, you see that tall dark cup of cappuccino? He's mine," she said. "You are not going to be the only one screwing this weekend, you watch!" She had made her mind up that it was going down this weekend. I looked at her and nervously rolled my eyes. The thought of her secretly going after Capone scared me.

She had his undivided attention and he looked over at her and smiled. They were creating subliminal messages right in the living room and the pheromones were flying! He propositioned her with his eyes and she accepted. I shook my head in total disapproval -- then their eyes locked, indicating that they had both blatantly chosen to ignore me. I was afraid of what would happen that weekend.

Chapter 19

An Escape to Nowhere

Paula talked about Capone the entire way to the club. When we pulled up to the hole-in-the-wall night club we both laughed, we'd be right at home because this is what we were used to. It reminded us of the Silk Carpet Lounge. We were new in this town and expected everyone to take notice when we walked in and that's exactly what they did. We stepped out of the car and held our heads high, and when we walked in everyone stared at us, one by one their eyes followed our every move. The men at the party couldn't break their stares and the women seemed envious. Timmy explained that people had heard we would be at the party and considered us "Chicago Girls," *good looking, shapely, and high class*. We laughed at the stereotype and wondered how you take a city and just assume that all of the women fall into one category.

Timmy made sure to let everyone know which of the "Chicago Girls" belonged to him. He kept his arm around my waist, and for most of the night he was at my side.

The party was packed and everyone was having a great time. I couldn't get past how people seemed to constantly stare at Timmy and I. Once again I reminded myself to drink up, party, and get on the road Sunday. Fran, Paula, and Wendy were dancing and creating a stir when I ran to join them on the dance floor.

"We them Chicago Girls!" we chanted as we laughed our way across the dance floor. We had danced so much that I sweated out my freshly straightened bob. My natural hair roots had reverted and were no longer compliant! I walked back to my seat, but Paula was still on the dance floor yelling, "Yeah, we them Chicago Girls!" Capone was sitting next to me enjoying every bit of her production. I politely walked out to the dance floor, "C'mon Missy you are drunk, and it's time to get out of here. Let's go." I found Timmy and the crew and we headed back to Capone's apartment.

Capone had walked into the living room and suggested we stay a couple more days. It had been a great weekend, but I knew the prolonged trip would cause my mother to be suspicious of our whereabouts. "I can't." "My mom is going to kill me if I don't get my sister back!"

The majority ruled, and in the end each of us agreed to stay a few more days so we could get it out of our system. Paula had made arrangements with her grandmother to take care of her son. It would be my task to make sure Capone didn't get his hands on Paula. Even with the apparent excitement, Timmy disappeared that morning without a word. He'd gotten up early and asked to borrow my car to go to the grocery store, but after several hours he still had not returned. I was worried because the car was in my brother's name. Now, Timmy had been gone for hours in the car that *wasn't* really my car. My mother and brother would kill me if they knew I'd let Timmy drive that car.

"Girl, something ain't right with that damn Timmy," Paula said. I knew what she was insinuating, but I hoped it wasn't true. We knew the signs all too well. I crossed my fingers and hoped that Timmy wasn't on drugs. 'Lord, please don't let this man be a drug addict.'

Timmy turned up later that evening explaining that he had been running errands for his mother and had run into old friends.

I was happy to have my car back safe and sound, but I knew that the situation could have turned out a lot worse. The following day we were sitting on the couch and there was a knock on the door.

"Is De'Vonna and Wendy here?" She stepped through the doorway and greeted me and I exchanged the greeting with apparent nervousness in my voice. My face was beet red from fear. Even though I considered myself an adult, I knew I would be in big trouble for bringing my younger sister to Rockford. Mama had always been resourceful, and though we were over a hundred miles away, she had found us. I knew she was upset, but she wasn't ranting and raving the way she normally did when we did something stupid. She had one purpose for being there and she was there to achieve that purpose only. There was nothing I could say that would justify my actions.

I imagined mama leaping across the room and grabbing me in my collar, so I positioned myself towards the back door and prepared my stance in case I needed to run. She sensed what I was thinking and said, "Don't run. Sit down. Stay right there. If I wanted to do something to you I could've done it by now, you've made your decision.

You want to be grown and I'm going to let you be grown, but you will not bring your sister down with you. Stay here as long as you like. I'm only here to pick up your sister. She will not turn out like you. Mama was completely calm as she motioned for my sister to rise from the couch. Go get your clothes Wendy, we're leaving." Wendy got up from the couch and went to retrieve all of her belongings without saying a word. Everyone sat in dead silence as my mother stood in the doorway with her lips pursed and her arms crossed, waiting for Wendy to return. Paula broke the silence when she looked at my mother and mustered up a hello. "Hey, Ms. Julie Ann, how you doing?" Mama pursed her lips tightly and scolded her, "Paula, you know, I've been better, but it don't make no sense how you left that boy with your grandmother. Yall are out here running around sleeping from pillar to post. Like some damn homeless dogs. Every one of you has a place to live. What kind of man allows a girl to travel over a hundred miles to see him and not have his own place." Then, she was done. My mother had a way of saying what she needed to say and bringing conviction to the receiver. Paula lowered her head in embarrassment and lied.

"I know, but we were planning to go home today," mama didn't believe it. "I bet you were," she shot back. My sister quietly descended the stairs with her clothes and belongings. As they headed toward the door Mama looked me straight in the eye. "You will get tired, I know you will. When you get *sick and tired*, you call me. I'm always here for you and I love you De'Vonna, but I will not chase you, this is *your* choice." There were no goodbye hugs or kisses. Mama was fed up with me and this time she'd chosen not to be driven by emotion. As far as she was concerned I'd become the prodigal daughter and when I was ready to come home she would accept me with open arms. As she walked out the door, I felt that I was denying the love I so desperately needed. My mother had a way of getting to me.

Timmy knew I was having a really hard time after my mother left, so he suggested we have a drink at a nearby bar. 'Maybe Timmy was the one. I'd have to take it slow and get to know him all over again.'

I could hear mama's words echoing in my head when Timmy pulled into a parking lot surrounded by rundown apartment buildings. She would be okay once I proved to her that I could be responsible. Her favorite line was, "Y'all need to be independent, don't wait on anyone else to take care of you, be independent." So, I'd show her that I could be independent, eventually.

"This ain't no bar. Where we at?" I asked. He explained that he needed to stop by his cousin's house and it would only take a few minutes. He got out of the car, looking to his left and then over his right shoulder.

Then, instinctively he lifted his hand, motioning for me to follow him out of the car. He'd made a split second decision. He knew leaving me in the car would not be a good idea. I imagined the headlines reporting, "Eighteen-year-old girl from Ford Heights, IL visits drug-ridden neighborhood and gets shot during robbery. No money was taken from the victim."

"Come on in with me, this won't take too long," he said. The building was three levels high, ash gray, and stained from years of harsh weather. Some windows were wide open and curtains waved in and out of the apartments from the brisk wind.

It was now winter, but many seasons of trash budded through the snow. I stepped over an empty bottle of Budweiser as we entered the apartment building. I shrieked at the condition of the interior and my heart pounded as I put myself on guard. I would be ready if someone tried to rob us. I was accustomed to these types of neighborhoods, but this was different. The destitution seemed even worse than Ford Heights.

When we entered the building I felt nauseated by the stench of urine that permeated the hallways. The paint was peeling off the walls and there were transients, drunks, and drug addicts laid out in the hallway floors. Timmy walked ahead of me, and when I reached out to place my hand on his back for comfort, he grabbed my hand, and I knew I'd be safe. "Don't worry its okay. I know everyone in this building." I wondered how he knew *everyone* in this building. We walked down the long hallway and finally approached the last door at the end of the hall. Timmy knocked on the door, and a light-skinned girl with dark circles under her eyes answered.

It was obvious that she'd been beautiful at some point in her life, but something had gotten a hold of her, and it was hanging on for dear life; strangling her, robbing her of her essence. I was familiar with this look and knew I was witnessing someone trapped in crack cocaine's clutches. I'd seen so many pretty girls get strung out on crack while their lives passed them by. "Wherrrrre you get herrrr from? She soooo pretty, Timmy," the girl slurred. "Thank you," I said shyly, forcing myself to smile and feeling ashamed of my apparent lack of sincerity. Thoughts whirled through my head. 'Who is this person, how does Timmy know her?' Timmy must have read my mind because he immediately introduced her as his cousin Tracy. My mind was at ease, but she looked like "death on a stick" as my godmother Sheila would say. The fact that she was his cousin made everything okay and I was instantly in a better mood. Maybe she was having problems, and Timmy was there to talk her through them.

"You can wait herrrrre...in the living room," she said, as she shoved the remote control into my chest and motioned for me to sit on the couch.

"I'll be right out," Timmy assured me as he followed his cousin into the bedroom.

Her apartment was fairly clean, but there wasn't much furniture, only the basic necessities – a lamp, couch, table, and two chairs. There were no pictures on the wall and the apartment didn't have a warm feeling like our old project had. Even though we were poor it always felt like home. 'Was Timmy selling drugs to her and didn't want me to know what he was up to? Yeah. That was probably it,' I thought. My rationalizations led me to believe that for sure the cousin was on drugs. But, Timmy…he was the drug dealer. And, that was fine with me. Regardless of what was going on I would pretend to be oblivious. I knew more about the streets than most boys my age, but I also knew enough to know that men liked it when you didn't seem to know anything about the fast life. Since Timmy thought I was innocent and pure I would oblige him. I smiled to myself and I did as I was told. I sat in front of the television and my heart was content, "Little House on the Prairie" was on.

Laura Ingalls was my favorite character and I couldn't be happier. Mary and Laura had just started school at Walnut Grove Junior High, and Laura was having a hard time with the new girl, Nellie.

I wished Laura would have kicked Nellie's snooty butt! If I was Laura, I wouldn't have taken that type of treatment from an arrogant student who was new to the school and the town!

I realized I'd been sitting on the couch for a full episode of Little House on the Prairie when I started nodding off. I sat up and felt like a dumb little girl. I wasn't a dumb girl. I was everything *but* that. Who did they think I was? I was from the projects! I instantly got angry, 'What the heck are they doing in there? If they are doing what I think they are doing in there I'm about to set it off in this place!' I got up from the couch and tiptoed to the door. I didn't hear any talking so I put my ear close enough to hear breathing. I pushed the door open quickly! The walls were bare without any sign of occupancy. The unmade tattered mattress had been shoved into the furthest corner of the tiny room without any thought.

The carpet was damaged and stained beyond normal wear and tear, clothes were scattered throughout the bedroom and paint was peeling off the walls. There was no dresser, night stand, reading lamp or any other furniture in the room.

As I began to make sense of what I'd just seen, the pungent smell quickly sunk into my nostrils. I'd smelled its scent before. It was powerful! Timmy was sitting on a red milk crate with a crack pipe in his mouth. He had been holding a lighter to it with one hand and holding the pipe to his lips with another. My hand was still on the door knob when I stepped backwards out of the room, "Oh my God! You're a crackhead! Oh my God! Oh my God!" I yelled. I couldn't believe what I'd just witnessed with my own eyes, I wanted to fight! I couldn't let this just happen like that. He'd made a complete fool out of me. I walked back into the room not knowing what I'd do. I had to make sure I'd seen it, and there it was lying on the floor, a glass crack pipe!

I paced back and forth across the room hitting my fist into the palm of my hand. "I can't believe you are a crackhead!

Lord, please tell me what I did to deserve a crackhead boyfriend?!" I couldn't believe this was happening. Tears streamed down my face, and every fiber in my body shook uncontrollably. "Take me back to the house Timmy! Take me back! You're a crackhead!" I screamed.

When Timmy dropped the crack pipe, his *cousin* frantically dropped to the floor on her hands and knees in a desperate attempt to retrieve every piece of crack that had fallen. I ran out of the apartment into the hallway, now blind to the destitution spread across the hallway floors. Timmy hurried behind me, "Come on now, it's no big deal! It was my first time. I promise, I have never done that before!" he screamed. I wasn't hearing it. Was that what he'd told girlfriends before me - that it was no big deal? His eyes glistened from the crack and the shock of being caught red-handed, "Please don't tell anyone," he begged as he grabbed my wrist. I stood outside the car devastated and in tears. "Just unlock the door," I cried. I couldn't look at him. He walked to the driver's side and unlocked the door.

The ride to his brother's house was filled with dead silence, no music, no talking. "I really messed up with you, didn't I?" Timmy asked. He searched for the right words, but he couldn't find any verbiage to erase what I'd seen and he knew it. As he drove me back to his brother's house I was forced to visualize the faces of everyone who looked at me with pity; all the people in the club that night.

Even Capone had known it. He thought that I'd be the one to help his brother change his life and help him to finally break free from his addiction. I thought back to the night we were in the nightclub and people whispered. They knew things about him that I didn't know, they all knew Timmy was a crackhead, and people simply felt sorry for the pretty "Chicago girl" who thought she had a prince charming. Maybe they had all wondered if my love for Timmy would break crack's hold.

'How long had he been on crack? How could I help him with an addiction that I knew nothing about? Had his mother sent him to live with his father years ago because he was addicted to crack?'

I had many questions, but I didn't need the answers. I shamefully reflected on what people may have thought or said about me. What do you think about a girl in a relationship with a crackhead? Only that she must already be one or she will be one soon.

When we returned to the house I ran upstairs and couldn't find Paula. I'd looked everywhere but in the basement. I was exhausted and my mind was blank. Just as I started packing my clothes Paula and Capone walked into the bedroom together. There was no one else in the house but them. It had finally happened. They had lasted a full ten days without having sex, and now they were both satisfied. Barbara was nowhere to be found. My mental state was fragile and I couldn't begin to entertain what had occurred between those two. I rolled my eyes and said, "Paula, we have to go. Timmy's a crackhead. I caught him smoking crack."

"Oh my God! I knew it, I knew it! I knew something was up with him," she said. There was now a connection between Capone and Paula that hadn't been there before. They looked into each other's eyes and it was clear that they were both saddened by my admission.

But, I'd seen something else when their eyes locked. They knew it was likely, that they would never see each other again.

Capone left the room and minutes later we heard him screaming at Timmy. "You have just lost the best thing that has ever happened to you, and you will never find a good woman like De'Vonna, you dumb ass!" "I know, I know, I know," Timmy replied, his voice full of shame and regret. I tuned them out and continued to pack my clothes.

I'd known and seen enough crack heads in my life to see the signs, but somehow I'd missed them in Timmy. The truth is, I didn't want to see it, and I didn't want to believe it. The dream I'd painted years ago of him and I getting married and having children was now shattered. I'd put my life on hold for him, including my relationship with my mother, which had been getting better before I decided to run away to Rockford. Someone knocked on the bedroom door.

"I don't want to talk to him," I told Paula, assuming it was Timmy. She smiled weakly as she opened the door. It was Capone.

"Can I talk to you, sis?" he asked.

"Yeah, sure…C'mon in," I said.

My eyes were swollen from crying. He embraced me and said, "Sister-in-law, I know we just met, but you are cool people. I love my brother, but he will never meet another woman like you. He really screwed up this time. You are the truth." I cried in his arms and wished it was my father who was there holding me. My father had not been involved in my life, ever. My mother didn't believe in "forcing a man to provide for his child."

He retired from a job that was less than three miles from where I grew up and every day he drove through the town where I lived and he never stopped. He fixed his brain to forget that I was ever born and it worked for him, but it sure didn't work for me. I didn't know what it was like to have a man love me and not want anything in return. Once again, I had to ask myself, when will someone love me? Capone had made me feel better, but I was sure I would never be back.

Timmy stood at the door with tears in his eyes. "Please don't leave," he begged. He knew that this was his last chance, and I'd never return, "Give me another chance De'Vonna, please?" He looked pitiful.

He'd been crying, but he understood the magnitude of what was happening. I'd made up my mind. I was not going to date someone who was addicted to crack. I'd seen too many lives shattered behind a crack addiction, and I was not signing up for that.

I could taste the salty tears dripping down my face, "This is one thing I won't settle for Timmy." I walked out the door and I was headed home. We didn't say much on the way home. We were all taking in the things that had occurred over the last month. We had been in Rockford for weeks, and I had chosen to ignore all the signs pointing to Timmy's addiction, but I couldn't ignore what I had seen with my own eyes. It was hard to imagine a nineteen-year-old man strung out on crack. How could that happen? That was the question that I struggled with during the long stretch on highway 94 back to Ford Heights. I'd closed another chapter in my life and I'd be moving forward, leaving thoughts of Timmy where they belonged, in my childhood.

Chapter 20

Prodigal Daughter

On the ride home I thought about my life and reflected on some of the choices I'd made. If I didn't start to fly right I was going to crash. I made up my mind that I was going to sign up for Operation 25, a program that allowed dropouts to go back to high school and get a diploma, but the first thing on my agenda was to be a better big sister. I'd be an example to my little sisters, that was what they needed right now, a positive role model and I was far from ready. It was time for me to grow up! I stopped by Mama's first because I hadn't seen China and Shanece in quite a while.

When I pulled into my mother's driveway, my sister China was standing outside with her friends bouncing a basketball through a make-believe hoop. She was eleven years old! I didn't realize how fast they were growing up until that moment. Before I could fully step out of the car China ran up to me and wrapped her arms around my neck.

She was so cute and had the biggest brown eyes I'd ever seen. I'd teased endlessly that I was going to pluck her eyes out since God didn't give them to me. That hug made me feel so loved. I stood outside and played ball with them for a few minutes before I went inside. Shanece, the younger of the two, was sitting in front of the television watching cartoons. She had four ponytails in her head and her hair needed to be combed. She was tall for a ten-year-old. She jumped up and down. "Heyyyyyyyyy sister! I missed you! Where you been?" I loved how oblivious little kids were. They loved me for who I was and had no idea the life I'd been living or the pain and anguish I'd caused our mother. I laughed and lifted her on my hip. She barely fit anymore. "Wow, you're a giant! What are they feeding you?" I walked to the bathroom to find the hair supplies. The barrettes, hair grease, and hair balls were in the usual spot. When I lived with Mama she never had to comb my sisters' hair. She was too busy working so I always did it, but lately I hadn't been home much. I kissed Shanece on her cheek. She jumped down onto the floor and sat between my legs. She knew the drill. I missed being a big sister, but that was going to change.

I wasn't sure if I'd be moving back to Mama's house or not, but I'd definitely start helping mama take care of my sisters and my younger brother.

Mama and Wendy had been at the Laundromat when I got to the house. As I was combing Shanece's hair I heard mama's car pull into the driveway. Wendy walked in the door first with two thirty gallon trash bags full of clean laundry and caught sight of me. I put my index finger to my lips to "shush" her. When Mama walked into the house and saw me combing my little sister's hair, her eyes widened, and she couldn't contain her emotions. She had been so preoccupied with lugging the laundry into the house that she didn't see my car parked across the street. She dropped the laundry basket she'd been holding, and with tears running down her cheeks, she grabbed me tight.

"Lord, thank You for bringing my baby home safe! God, I love you! You answered my prayers! Thank you Lord Jesus!" Mama had been on a seven-day fast believing that God would bring me home. She didn't ask any questions when she walked over to me, wrapped her arms around me and held on tight.

She rocked me slowly in her arms as she wept. I'd grown up too fast and mama reminisced back to the day she first brought me home from the hospital. All she saw was a beautiful five pound infant, a tiny little girl that she'd be bringing home from St. James Hospital, her first born daughter. I was eleven months old when my sister was born, the regrets were paramount, and mama rocked me harder, wishing she never had to let me go, "My baby," mama cried. "I'm sorry baby," I'm sorry for it all. Then, she thanked God through her tears. Mama had a way of making each of us feel as if we were the apple of her eye. My mother had loved and accepted me in spite of my ways.

From my peripheral vision, I saw an object flip in mid air. It was my little brother Ron Jr. wearing Spiderman pajamas. He had so much energy, but he was an introvert and played alone. That worried some adults, but he was smarter than most kids his age and even some adults.

"Get over here and give me a hug, I know you see me," I said. Ron ran over, hugged me tight, and then kissed me on the cheek.

He then got a running start and flipped over the couch. Mama looked at him sternly and said, "Boy, if you don't get up and take a shower, you better!"

He hopped up from the floor, and we all laughed. Mama wanted to be angry at him for jumping and flipping in the house, instead she laughed and pointed towards the bathroom and Ron knew that it was time to take a shower. 'Home sweet home,' I thought.

The following Monday Paula and I enrolled in Operation 25. We were so excited that things were looking up for us. I moved back home and was there most of the time, but I still spent the weekends at Paula's. She had started seeing Derrick on a regular basis and he was always at her house. I'd gotten several messages from Napoleon while we were in Rockford, but I hadn't seen him in almost eight months. I'd made it clear to all of my friends that they weren't supposed to even mention his name in my presence.

The first day at Operation 25 was a cinch. We took assessments and were assigned curriculum at our appropriate reading and math levels. I'd have all the credits that I needed in no time. School was going really well, and I was elated to rediscover my love for writing.

The English teacher assigned us a project, which required that we write a twenty-page "mini-book" on any subject. My manuscript ended up being about a girl that had been on a fast track to the gutter and was going downhill quickly. I was proud of my manuscript and handed it over to Mrs. Olson with glee. The next morning she met me at the classroom door.

"De'Vonna, can I see you in my office, please?"

I followed her into her office as she closed the door behind us. She had taken my writing home that night and read it in its entirety and was visibly distraught.

"De'Vonna, if this person is you, you really need to seek help. You have been through a lot and I'm deeply worried about you. You should never have had to experience the things you wrote about." I didn't quite understand the magnitude of what I had written or that there had been anything dysfunctional about most of what I'd written about. Most people went through these things, right? *Wrong*, "not most, De'Vonna, but a lot of people do experience sexual violence or abuse," my teacher confirmed. She was from a suburban, white family and she admitted that it had even happened in her family.

Although it was quite sobering to hear her truths, I wasn't ready to disclose mine, nor was I ready to open up to someone who was so different from me, and everyone around me. "This *person,* I wrote about is not me." I lied.

I had created a therapeutic out by writing about my life story and expected that a reader would understand and accept it as entertainment. My life had been far from entertaining. I'd grown up too fast, and so had everyone around me.

Chapter 21

A Wolf in Sheep's Clothing

I'd spent the weekends at Paula's after we returned from Rockford. One night after falling asleep on her couch I was awakened by the doorbell. Though it was Saturday night I wasn't expecting anyone. The doorbell sounded continuously. I dragged myself from the couch assuming it was Paula and Derrick returning from the popular sandwich restaurant, Big Boys. "Where is your key?" I said, as I struggled to find the light. I had gone to bed early and couldn't believe this girl had left her key! I looked out the peephole, but couldn't see anything because she had strategically placed her hand over the peephole. "Stop playing, girl, I'm too sleepy for this crap." I snatched the door open, ready to give her a verbal lashing, and froze in place. I couldn't move. It was Napoleon! How did he know where to find me? I'd been living at my mom's house, but he would never have the nerve to knock on my mother's door. Mama hated him with a passion.

"What the hell do you want?" The words vehemently escaped my lips.

"I just had to see you. I haven't seen you in so long. I haven't been able to do anything but think about you since you left. I love you baby, I do." I stood in front of the door with my hands on my hips waiting to hear something more believable than what he'd just said. I evaluated the package that stood before me. He wore a white jogging suit with his name embroidered on the front of the jacket. He wasn't tall; in fact, he was less than six feet. He'd picked up some weight and was pudgy. His complexion was light brown with deep red undertones. He wasn't handsome, but had a boyish baby face which made him easier to forgive. The Drakkar cologne he wore enthralled me, and he was irresistible standing in the doorway. Once again, I could feel myself slipping under his spell, but I couldn't let him just walk back into my life as if nothing had happened. I fought off the obsession.

"What the hell do you want, Napoleon? I don't want you. I'm done with you." He lowered his head and instantly looked pitiful; it was *that look* that always got to me. "Baby, I love you. Just let me hold you. I know I hurt you, I know I did, but I won't do it again. Let me take care of you," he begged.

"No, no, no. We have been through this before," I said. My emotions took control and I choked up. By then, Napoleon had stepped into the apartment and put his arms around me. I dropped my head into his chest and wept, tears streamed down my face. Seeing him had weakened all my defenses. I thought I was over him. "I hate you, I really do. I hate you. I hate the ground you walk on. You don't love me. You don't know how to love me," I whispered. I didn't fight his kisses or his caress. I couldn't. What I had vowed not to do again, I had done. And, once again, things were back to the way they had been before I left. It was our normal. We were secretly spending time together as if we hadn't missed a beat. The feelings that I had buried had erupted like volcanic material and were more intense than ever.

Paula and I were sitting in her apartment when we heard loud music outside her window. The bass was bumping, and Heavy D and the Boyz's "We Got Our Own Thang" was banging from the speakers. I could hear the music beating in my chest. The windows were vibrating from the bass. Paula turned towards the window, rolled her eyes and hissed.

"That's Napoleon," she said. "And real men knock on the door." I ignored her disdain for him and jumped on the couch that faced the window to make sure it was him. When I saw the black Cadillac with tinted windows and 18" rims I ran to the door. My cousin *Damien* got out of the car. He walked up the side walk, reached for the door handle and walked inside the apartment before either of us could invite him in. I moved away from the door when he entered, I had not forgotten what he'd done. "What's up cousin?" he asked. I pretended not to hear him. I'd heard that he had been hanging out with Napoleon these days. As he walked towards the door my stomach churned. Every time I saw him, I wanted to puke. I didn't respond to his greeting, instead I walked towards Paula's bedroom. "Napoleon wants you to come out to the car," he said. I went into the bathroom to take the pink rollers out of my head and to fix myself up a little. I quickly applied eyeliner and mascara to make my eyes pop, took one last look in the mirror, and was satisfied. I headed outside. I found it strange that he didn't come in, but then I remembered he was dropping off the money he'd promised and probably had to go take care of some of his drug business.

I'd seen the most beautiful leather jacket with a blue fox collar downtown in the window and had fallen in love with it. I excitedly called Napoleon to tell him how much I really wanted it and he had promised that he would get it for me that week. I got even more excited thinking about the coat.

I approached the car, but couldn't see through the tinted windows, so I stood in front of the window and leaned in closer with a big smile on my face. The back window slowly rolled down, and to my dismay, Sassy and Napoleon were both in the back seat. I was perplexed. 'What was this?!' I thought. Napoleon glared directly into my eyes and began speaking. "Listen here, De'Vonna, I want you to stop calling my phone, do not send people looking for me or asking me for money! I'm getting married, and Sassy is going to be my wife. Leave us alone, do you hear me you little bitch?!" My heart felt like it had broken into a thousand tiny pieces. I couldn't speak. I was literally immobile. I wanted to run, but my feet would not move. I couldn't talk for several seconds. 'How could he do something like that to me?

Who was this person?' I had never seen this side of Napoleon before. I was finally seeing the snake that everyone had accused him of being. Sassy didn't say a word, instead she laughed, and I could tell by the expression on her face that she was enjoying every minute of it. I was enraged and visibly shaken, but without hesitation, I transformed from the young, sweet, calm girl to a woman scorned. There was no way I would allow him to treat me like that in front of anyone. I leaned closer into the car and focused my attention solely on Napoleon while tuning Sassy out. I'd gotten a burst of courage from deep within and I was going to deal with him once and for all.

"I was minding my own business Napoleon and you came and found me. You can do what you want, you can say what you want, you can marry *who* you want, but I am pregnant with OUR child, and you will take care of it." Napoleon looked at Sassy and was adamant, "she lying Sassy, I aint been with her and she aint pregnant by me." I leaned closer into the car and looked directly at Napoleon, "We have been sleeping together since I got back in town and now you try to make it appear as if I was stalking you?

You found me. You tracked me down. Now I will find *you* to make sure you pay your child support because you and I, well…. we's having a baby. See you in court, baby daddy!!"

The three of us had taken pregnancy tests that morning, and each of them had come back positive! Fran, Paula and I were all going to have babies. I had planned to tell Napoleon about my pregnancy after I went to the doctor. I never imagined I'd angrily disclose my pregnancy to him in front of Sassy. This was all too much for me. I suddenly didn't feel well. I'd gotten their attention and Sassy's expression had changed, she wasn't laughing any more and Napoleon was suddenly quiet. I turned and headed into Paula's apartment.

"Let's go, Damien," Napoleon said. My cousin never looked up at me. He had walked to the driver's side of the car while the commotion was in full force and I hadn't noticed he was now sitting in the car. A chauffer. I wasn't surprised at all. A "stool pigeon." That's what we called his *kind* in the projects. He drove off, and in seconds they were gone.

I'd put on my best face for Napoleon, Sassy, and my traitor cousin, but I was hurt beyond words.

I'd been punched in my stomach and I had no air supply, my feet were heavy and every step a burden. I went into the house to tell Paula what had just occurred. She was livid. "Oooooh, I hate that gay ass Napoleon! Listen here, I'm telling you De'Vonna, if you EVER take that gay bastard back, you dumb as hell!" I'd never agreed with Paula more. I'd be dumb as hell if I ever took him back.

Napoleon's cousin Nisa had come to Paula's house to fight me the very next day. Nisa was a tomboy and had a reputation for being a trouble maker. She and I had always been cordial to each other, so there was no real reason for her to justify fighting me. *Someone* was not happy that I would give birth to Napoleon's baby. Was he really that lowdown that he'd pay someone to try and make me lose my baby? I didn't want to believe that, but based on the previous day's events I would never put anything past Napoleon again. I had never been afraid of a fight and in this case, a lot was at stake, I had to fight her. This girl was known around town for initiating fights or being paid to settle a score. So when she knocked on the door and asked me to come outside I knew what I had to do.

She bullied people all through junior high and had gotten suspended countless times for fighting. People did not pick fights with Nisa. She had garnered such a reputation for being a bad ass that people had started contracting her services. Regardless of her reputation, I was going to defend myself. One thing that I knew for sure was that there was no way she was going to come looking for me and not get a good fight. I walked out of the door, but before I could make it to the porch Paula had come running in front of me.

"Look here, Nisa, I need to check yo' pockets before y'all fight because this has got to be a fair fight." Nisa rolled her eyes at Paula and told her to "stay out of it."

"Well, y'all ain't fighting until you empty your pockets," Paula said. She meant those words, and in a sense I knew she felt responsible for me. Nisa had been known to fight unfairly with knives and brass knuckles so this was not an unreasonable request. She emptied out her pockets and brass knuckles fell out.

"Okay, what else you got?" Paula asked with an accusing look. Nisa emptied the rest of her pockets, and she was clean. She took off her coat, and I stepped out the door. It was the middle of February and the cold wind was brisk that day.

I took off my jacket, and before Nisa could get into her stance I rushed her. I punched her dead in her nose and we were both throwing "hay makers!" She had my hair wrapped around her hand, and I kneed her in the stomach to get her to release my hair. She fell to the ground, and I landed on top of her with my legs spread apart as she lay beneath me. I jabbed her in the face and she reached up with both hands and dug her fingernails deep into my face repeatedly. She was larger than I was, but I was fast. I had older brothers and they "rough housed" and wrestled with us girls all the time. I knew how to fight, but only when I had to. She tried to throw punches, but her body was locked beneath me and she couldn't move. I learned this move from my mother years ago. "If you ever get into a fight, get on top and put your knees on their shoulders; they won't be able to move."

Mama didn't advocate fighting, but she knew that where we were from, it was inevitable. She wanted to make sure that we knew how to protect ourselves. Nisa's sister had seen enough. Her sister was on the bottom and wasn't coming up anytime soon. She finally broke it up without jumping in.

As Nisa found her way off the ground she ran for me and before I knew it, she had dead-locked her teeth into my neck. I screamed for dear life! I could feel the warmth of my blood dripping down my neck as she held my hair in a tight grip. I could tell that she was summoning up more strength, she didn't imagine I'd put up such a fight—and now she was really mad! I jabbed her in the eye twice and she released my hair from her grip. Both of her eyes were swollen, and my neck was throbbing, I knew that I would need a tetanus shot!

Her sister had stood by and watched us fight. She'd known better than to jump in because my family welcomed a fight, and that would not go over well once everyone found out. Paula and I went inside her house to grab our purses and head to the hospital. I had deep scratches all over my face, but I was enraged and ready to fight all night if that's what it took to earn respect. The next time we fought, I would be the initiator. I grabbed the cocoa butter and rubbed it on my face, as I vowed to finish Nisa off whenever and wherever I saw her. It was not over, pregnant or not.

Just as I had expected, not even a week later, Paula and I were riding through The Bronx, and saw Nisa standing outside talking with friends as if nothing had happened. She didn't see us. We quickly drove to Paula's house knowing that we had to move fast before Nisa left. I jumped out of the car and ran inside. I'd strategically been storing a two-by-four behind Paula's front door especially for Nisa! I took off running on foot. To my delight and relief, Nisa was still standing in the same spot with her back turned, I raised the two-by-four above her head and brought it down with a force that sounded with a crack. The wood split in half.

"Oh my God! Oh, my God!" she screamed." Someone go get my sister, Chessie!"

"Be bad now! Where's your posse now!" I yelled. "You can get whoever you like, but the next time somebody put out a hit on me, you better give their money back!"

Paula and I headed back to her apartment, and less than an hour later, a mob had gathered outside her front windows. Minutes later gun shots poured into her apartment.

Paula and I quickly scurried to the floor. We were terrified and did our best to keep quiet. As we lay on the floor afraid for our life, Paula crawled into her bedroom and snatched the phone from the night stand. She dialed 911 and screamed into the phone, "there are people shooting into my apartment, we need help!"

When the police arrived ten minutes later the mob had already dispersed. They took a report and drove us to my mother's house, we would be safe there. Everyone knew where my family lived, but Nisa and her family wouldn't dare come there. I came from one of the largest families in town; you didn't play with the Bentleys. Paula and I treaded very carefully and watched our backs for the next few months, but I'd heard that Nisa vowed to let it go until I'd given birth to my baby.

Chapter 22

A Good and Perfect Gift

My stomach was protruding and I had found something else to love. I was in love with the baby growing in my belly. Mama and I were in the grocery store one day and I felt a flutter in my stomach. I was still embarrassed to express to anyone that I liked being pregnant. "Mama, I just felt something move in my stomach." Mama was an expert in this field, she'd given birth to seven children. "Well, you are pregnant, I suppose that would be the baby," she said, and we both laughed. I'd finally felt connected to something. I went to the library and checked out books because I heard that if you read to your baby while they were still in the womb it increased their intelligence. I listened to music and talked to my little angel. I hoped it was a boy, but I wanted the sex of my baby to be a surprise.

After Mama had gotten over the shock and disappointment of me being pregnant at eighteen she was quick to defend me when people criticized me for being a teen mom. She would say, "Well at least she's eighteen. She ain't the first, and she won't be the last."

Mama decorated the basement room for me and the baby. I had gone from 110 lbs to 155 lbs, my feet were swollen, and I could barely walk. Fran, Paula and I would all have her babies two weeks apart! I was glad that I didn't have to endure a pregnancy alone. I spent a lot of time thinking about my life and making plans for the future. My emotions were up and down, but overall I had a happy pregnancy and I had declared that this baby would be happy too. Napoleon had been telling everyone that my baby was "the community-baby." I held my head up and tried to ignore the things that I'd heard. I had to keep moving. I couldn't stop to think about anyone but the baby I was carrying in my belly. I was eight months pregnant the day Napoleon and Sassy got married. I had talked to him twice during my pregnancy. He had called and begged me to have an abortion early in my pregnancy.

"I will not kill my baby! I don't need you Napoleon. Besides, this is the *community's baby*, remember?" I slammed the phone down. The other time he called me was on the night of his bachelor party. I could hear loud music and women laughing in the background.

"So, you're really going to do it?" I asked him. "I love you De'Vonna," he said. "You don't love me, Napoleon. You love her. You have never loved me," I replied. He pleaded with me to see him that night. "There are strippers here," he said, "but I don't want to be here. I want to be with you. Please. If you come, I won't marry her tomorrow, I promise." I could no longer hear the background noise and knew he'd gone into another area of the house. "This time things will be different." I heard the desperation in his voice. "I love you. Please, I just want to talk to you, I have to see you. Please. I will not marry her if you come to me tonight. I promise you, I've never been so serious in my life. I love you, I'm sorry for everything. You should hate me." At that moment I felt deeply empty. I had no more tears left. I couldn't mourn or grieve what we never really had in the first place. There was nothing left. As much as I loved him, I couldn't do it. I could not allow myself to be sucked in by his lies and deceit. I'd had enough of his promises. This time I wasn't hearing it. I was carrying his child, and I'd been ridiculed by him. There was nothing in me that wanted to see him.

"You have hurt me so many times, but this time I can't give you the satisfaction. Go get married Napoleon," and I slammed the phone down in his ear. Within ten minutes the phone rang again, he was not giving up. When I answered the phone, I realized it was Lucas' voice on the other end. Apparently, Napoleon had offered him a large sum of money to convince me to see him. "What is going on with you and Napoleon?" Lucas asked. "Nothing," I replied, as my voice trembled and my emotions defied me. Though I had fought the tears when I talked to Napoleon, I was now crying uncontrollably. "I'm so tired of him Lucas, all he's ever done was hurt me. He means me no good. I can't see him."

My friend regretted making the call for Napoleon, "I'm on my way over there right now," he had heard the pain in my voice. When Lucas walked into my mom's house he put his arms around me and assured me that it would be okay. I pushed him away because I needed to know, "Are you going to the wedding?" I asked.

"D, you *know* this is political, I have to go, you know that, but, I hope you are really done with him this time," he said before leaving.

My heart was broken, but I felt strong knowing that I'd stood up for what I believed in. Finally. I made a decision based on what was best for me and my child.

Napoleon and Sassy were married the next day. To add insult to injury, they brought a parade of cars past my house to prove to me that they had really done it. I was sitting in my mom's living room when I heard continuous horns blowing and people cheering from the cars as they rode by. Air raced from my lungs and I searched for oxygen. I imagined myself standing up in the church when the preacher asked, "Is there anyone here who sees just reason why these two should not be joined together in holy matrimony?"

"Me, Reverend, me! Napoleon will never be faithful. Not to Sassy, not to anyone!" He had really married her. I couldn't move. I hated him, and I hated her. Maybe that's what needed to happen. Maybe he needed to marry her so I could move on with my life. Tears stung my eyes. *She* was now officially Mrs. Napoleon Harris. I couldn't sleep for days.

Chapter 23

Blessing after the storm

I groaned from the intense pain, but I would not cry. No matter how much it hurt I wouldn't cry. Having a baby wasn't so bad if you imagined being in a field with purple flowers. It was happening. I was going to give birth, and I was going to be a mother.

'Where is Dr. Oluwago?' I wondered. The welfare insurance card was referred to as the "green card," and was only accepted by certain physicians. Dr. Oluwago was one of the few physicians who accepted *our* insurance plan. Every young mother I knew was Dr. Oluwago's patient. There were always rows of teen mothers waiting to see him when I went to my appointments. He had delivered most of the children in Ford Heights, and several of the girls joked about how "he done seen all of our private parts." Dr. Oluwago was from Africa and had a booming practice in Chicago Heights. He had prepared me for labor with his thick "straight-from-the-mother land" accent.

"When dee pains come, count dee contractions and when dey are less den five minutes apahht, you are to go to dee hospitell."

I had timed my contractions. The first one started at ten o'clock, and I'd gotten out of the bed to grab a pencil so I could make a note of the next one; it had come at ten-twenty, and they increased from there. All I saw were purple flowers and now they were poking through the ground, growing profusely. The ground was covered with purple flowers.

Mama had packed my *hospital* bag with outfits, pampers, and sleepers for the baby months earlier. She threw in clothes, sanitary napkins, toothbrush, and pajamas for me. As my delivery date got closer, mama made a habit of going through the bag often to make sure I hadn't added or taken things that I would need at the hospital. She had started working at a residential house taking care of developmentally delayed adults. Mama had already told her boss that her daughter's due date was close and she wanted to be there when the baby was born.

"Okay, okay, start timing your contractions."

"I did already, Mama.

"Are you in pain?"

"Kind of, but I'm okay, Mama."

"You are having a baby, what do you mean you're okay? Maybe you're not really in labor."

"Yes, I am, Mama, my water bag busted; I am in labor."

"Okay, wake your brother up and have him take you to the hospital. Big Mama and I will meet you there." My grandmother had already reserved her spot in the delivery room. Whenever she could witness the birth of her great grandchildren she did. I wobbled downstairs and opened my brother's door. He was asleep when I yelled into his room.

"Bryce, my water bag busted and I think the baby is coming!" He jumped out of the bed frantically.

"Well damn, what you want me to do?"

"A ride to the hospital would be nice." I forced a smile on my face, "Brother, you have to take me to the hospital or I'm going to have this baby right here in front of you." My brother didn't want me to know it, but he had a funny way of showing his emotions. I think he was pretty honored to be driving me to the hospital. He jumped out of the bed and was ready in no time. The hospital was about twenty minutes away, right down the main freeway connecting Ford Heights to surrounding areas.

My brother must have been driving at about ninety miles per hour when we got pulled over by a police officer. He seemed a little nervous, but looked over at me and said, "You better start screaming and hollin' as if that damn baby coming out now!" As soon as the police walked to the car, I panted and breathed harder than I needed to. My brother co-signed and explained to the officer that I was in labor. "Okay, follow me," the officer said. My brother followed the officer, while he managed the traffic ahead of us and made a clear pathway to the hospital. We entered St. James Hospital through the emergency room and I was immediately taken to the maternity ward. Several hours later, Dr. Oluwago had delivered my beautiful, healthy baby.

"It's a little girl," the nurse said, by then everyone in the room was crying. I turned toward my mother and tears streamed from my eyes. "Mama, I have a baby girl. I'm a mother. I'm a mother." Mama smiled. "Yes, you are, and you will be a great mother. I know you will. You did such a great job honey," she was so proud of me and I knew it. She kissed me on my cheek and embraced me. Dr. Oluwago held my baby girl as she screamed at the top of her lungs.

He passed her to the nurse to get cleaned up, and when the nurse was finished she laid her on my chest.

"Oh, Mama, she is so beautiful, so precious. I love her so much." I was no longer a girl, I was a woman. I now had to be responsible for another human being, I had to grow up. There would be no more running away or disappearing for weeks at a time. I kissed my baby and gave mama the honor of naming my first born child, Brittany. She was seven pounds, eleven ounces, beautiful, and had a head full of thick hair. She looked just like Napoleon. I instantly felt sad. I was placed in the welfare ward which consisted of two to four teen moms sharing a room. There was no privacy when visitors came, but many of my friends had children already and were familiar with this set up.

The next day several visitors came to the hospital to see me. Even though I knew all of them, some of them were "secret agents" sent to see what the baby looked like. Napoleon attempted to reach me after the baby was born. He offered to send money or to come see Brittany, but I declined. I'd been through too much, and I couldn't allow myself to go backwards because I'd made too much progress.

My family was ecstatic about the birth of my daughter. My mother handpicked Brittany's godparents. I was already a godmother at seventeen, but my mother was not having that. She was adamant that Brittany's godparents would be a married couple, stable and in a position to take care of her if there was ever a need. Billie Joe and Mama Flower loved my baby as much as we did. Mama had chosen the right couple. They had six sons and no daughters and Brittany was the apple of their eye.

Brittany, 6 Months Old

Chapter 24

Evolution of Transformation

One night as I lay in the bed next to my six month old daughter, I looked over on the night stand and noticed her baby book. I picked it up and flipped through the pictures. I didn't want her life to be like mine. I flipped to a blank page in the back of the book and started writing, I made my requests known to the Lord and I prayed He would hear me and honor my prayer.

Dear Lord,

Today is May 24, 1991 and I hope and pray that you make a way so that Brittany will be raised to love more than what I had and be more than what mom was. always will she mean the world to me. She deserves the best and so did me and her grandmother but all things are done for a reason. Lord Please find a reason.

Love Pam

I felt better after writing. I could always find an escape in writing. As I closed the book and put it away, I knew that God would respond. Things were working out at Mama's house, and we were all in love with the baby. Bryce had his own special nickname for Brittany. He called her "cabbage patch" because he thought she looked like a Cabbage Patch doll. She started walking when she was nine months old, and we all knew she would be a fast learner. 'Must have been all that reading I did when she was in my belly,' I'd say. I enjoyed having a baby and I savored every moment with her. I'd sit on the porch and laugh at Brittany's reaction to the passing cars.

One day as we sat on the porch our neighbor Santiago pulled into the driveway and got out of his car. "How come you never talk to me?" he asked. He was 6'3," brown-skinned, slim, and an average looking guy. I looked at him and laughed, "Probably because you don't know how to hold a decent conversation." He wasn't offended by my comment, in fact the more I tried to repel him, the more he hung on to my every word.

He begged me to attend a New Years party with him, "It's not like you have something else to do." He was right I didn't have anything else going on. I hadn't been to a club or to a party in almost a year so I was secretly looking forward to going. I knew people would start rumors about Santiago and me, so I decided to take my chances. I didn't care what people thought anymore.

When we arrived at the VFW Hall for the party, the lot was packed. This was much nicer than the other spots in town so I knew people would be dressed up. My body had snapped right back into shape after Brittany was born and I was proud of my new "grown lady curves," but I wouldn't be wearing the usual scandalous outfits that I was known for. I'd gone out and specifically bought a dress for the occasion, a classic white halter dress, very becoming of a young woman evolving. I looked in the mirror before I left and had to do a double take, I was definitely my mother's child. It was amazing how much I'd started to look like her. Before I left I stopped by mama's room to show her what I was wearing, but she wasn't there. I sprayed on some of her Sand & Sable perfume and kissed Brittany goodnight.

My little sisters would be babysitting and Santiago had promised to pay them.

When Santiago knocked on the door he was looking dapper, wearing black dress pants with a striped black and white dress shirt and shiny black Stacy Adams shoes. "You almost look cute," I said as we both broke into gut wrenching laughter. I laughed even harder when he couldn't get rid of that silly grin.

When we pulled up to the party I saw people I hadn't seen in a long time. I ran into some old friends and stood around chatting about old times. It felt good to be out. There were mostly older people at the event and I was perfectly okay with that. I missed Paula and Fran and suddenly felt sad that we had grown apart and made new friends. I hadn't seen them since we said our goodbyes at Fran's going away party months earlier. It still made my heart a little weak when I realized that she had relocated to Minnesota. "Who wants to move to "cold ass Minnesota?" we asked. We were still in touch, that hadn't changed, but as life would have it we were all doing our own thing.

As I reminisced about old times with the girls, couples began to step! Steppin' defined a unique style of dance and culture in many black communities.

It was a type of dance that older black folks treasured. It is to black folks what waltzing is to white folk. I enjoyed watching people step! I watched the veterans move to the stepping music. That's the one thing I knew I'd always love about home. There was simply nothing as relaxing and enjoyable as watching people dance to good, old-fashioned R&B; the old kind of R&B that made you smile and feel good inside.

It was easy to tell which of the couples were either married, had been stepping together for years, or had just met that night. There was an unbelievable connection when married people stepped; their moves were seamless. They'd been through good times and bad times, they had maybe been close to divorce, had dealt with sickness, death of loved ones, and other tragedies, but they made it. It showed in their dance. When strangers tried to find their groove on the dance floor they were clumsy and couldn't seem to quite get it right. Then there were the people who weren't married, but had frequented the same places and learned how to dance with each other by finding their flow. These were the real pros because they could get out on the dance floor with another veteran and make stepping look easy.

I stepped with a couple of people throughout the evening because Santiago had two left feet and couldn't dance at all.

When we left the party a guy angrily confronted Santiago. "What's up now, punk? What's all that stuff you were talking?" I didn't peg Santiago as the type of guy to be involved in drama. It was simply not him. I grabbed his arm and said, "Let's go, it's not worth it." Besides, I was dressed up, and I didn't feel like fighting or trying to break up a fight between two dudes. Santiago passed me the keys and demanded that I "Go to the car." I was irritated, "let's just go!" I yelled. I walked to the car and left them standing on the sidewalk arguing. I was a new mom, and I didn't have time for it. I slid into the driver's side of the car and put the keys in the ignition. "Uhhh! I am looking too cute for this, and I am getting too old for this, too," I said out loud. There was no one there but me, I laughed at how much I sounded like my mother. I backed Santiago's car out of the parking space and pulled to the front of the building to wait for him to come out. Just as I put the car in park Santiago approached the driver's side running in full speed, he fell and almost slid underneath the car.

He quickly recovered from the fall, ran to the passenger side, opened the door, and jumped in. "Drive! Drive as fast as you can!" he yelled. I sped off as fast as I could, but the car wasn't moving fast enough to get away from the bullets that flew in and around the car! Several bullets hit the car. I kept my head low as I drove in and out of lanes trying to avoid hitting the cars that were coming towards us. "Oh my God!" I screamed. "What is this about?!" My hands shook and I could barely hold the steering wheel straight. Santiago let down the passenger side window, leaned out the car, and started shooting back. "Oh my God!" I screamed. "I'm going to die in this car! I have a daughter to live for! I can't do this! Oh God, please don't let me die in this car tonight!" I had to think fast. I knew the police station was on the next block so I made a quick turn into the parking lot. The car kept right past us.

"Follow that car!" Santiago yelled.

"I'm not following that car, are you crazy?!" I yelled at him. Santiago explained that he had been dealing drugs, but had recently stopped and the guy was upset because it affected his sales.

When Santiago dropped me off at home I looked in on Brittany, she was still sleeping safe and sound. I wanted to get away from Ford Heights, and the urge had become greater after I became a mother.

Santiago and I were spending a lot of time together, but we had never let on that we'd shared a secret moment of passion. We agreed that it couldn't happen again. I was on the rebound, and raising a young child. I didn't need another guy in my life.

I hadn't told anyone that Napoleon had called, and after numerous attempts of begging and pleading with me, I finally allowed him to see Brittany. I knew I couldn't justify it, but I wanted him to see our daughter. My family was very angry about how he had publicly denied Brittany, so I couldn't tell anyone that I wanted him to see her, to see how much she looked like him, like both of us. He had climbed through my basement window and come into my bedroom. That night he held her, kissed her, and out of his own mouth, he had said it, "She looks just like me, she looks like us." My heart melted as he held our child. I'd forgiven him for all the things he'd said and done, but I was moving on. God had answered my prayer and I was no longer in love with Napoleon.

I was set to graduate from Operation 25 in a couple of months and still hadn't found a place to live. I had finally concluded that I did not want to raise my daughter in Ford Heights. I'd seen enough and I had been through enough. My mission in life would be to raise my child in a better environment. Her battles would be different, she would only have to be a child and enjoy life's joys. I'd worry about everything else, and I'd make sure she was protected and safe. She wouldn't need any man to give her anything because I would give it to her.

My graduation from Operation 25 was a pinnacle moment and it got me to thinking and believing I could accomplish other things. Although it wasn't a "real" graduation, it was the conclusion of the De'Vonna Bentley saga, and I was moving into another phase of my life.

I'd had an epiphany when I walked across the stage. I cried when my name was called, "De'Vonna Lynn Bentley." At that point, it was as if God Himself had called my name. I had finally done it. 'I was a high school graduate.' When I looked in the audience and saw my mother holding my baby, it made me proud that I'd crossed the threshold, I'd gotten my diploma.

I'd gotten it a year later than my class, but I hadn't given up and that was all that mattered.

After graduating from Operation 25 my cousin suggested I enroll in a secretarial school with her so she wouldn't have to commute to downtown Chicago alone. It was something that I'd always wanted to do so I decided to give it a try. We took the trek downtown and registered at Catherine College in the summer of 1991 with no assistance from either of our parents. Most of the financial aid forms were filled out in the tiny office by a secretary. Once all of the paperwork was filled out we were both officially enrolled and told we'd be starting classes the following Monday. The commute to the college was two hours and thirty minutes each way including two bus transfers and a train ride into downtown.

I learned how to use shorthand, type, write professional letters, and how to dictate. But, after a couple of months of commuting I couldn't justify the costs of taking the bus and the train when there wasn't much more I could learn in that arena. After the second trimester, everything they taught us had become redundant so I quit.

I'd been thinking about moving out of state and the desire was becoming more of a reality every day. I'd been verbalizing it and mentally preparing myself for the move. Fran had moved to Minnesota and seemed to be doing quite well. We didn't believe her when she said she was moving, but she had done it and I knew I could too.

"If you come here you will find a good job and make a decent salary, and the schools here are so much better," she said. I had dreams and goals and I believed God heard prayers and I'd been praying, "Lord, this earth is yours and all the riches in it. If it is *not* for me to move to Minnesota, please allow things to fall in place here. If I don't find something within six months, Lord, I will take that as your sign that I *need* to move." I knew God had the power to make things fall into place even if my destiny wasn't in Minnesota. From that point on, I went on a massive search for a job and an apartment. I looked in Ford Heights and Chicago Heights because I knew I couldn't afford to live in the suburbs or anywhere else until my situation changed.

Sandra had become a young mother too and she was pregnant with her second child. She and I both were looking for an apartment and sharing information.

From the time I prayed and asked God, I'd really been speaking into existence what was already predestined, but it was a somber moment when I told mama I was moving to Minnesota.

"Are you sure you want to go?" She asked. "You don't have to go baby, you can just stay here, but I had made my mind up. "Yes, Mama, I want to go, I have to go.

I prayed and asked God to open the door if it was to be and to close it if it wasn't. Mama, He done kicked the door wide open. God's got me mama." My mother cried and held me tight as she prayed for God to keep me safe. "Lord Jesus, bless my child. Send the angels to encamp around her. God, give her the wisdom to come home if things aren't going right for her in Minnesota, and Lord, please take care of my grandchildren."

I was now three months pregnant with Santiago's child. I hadn't told him yet because we hadn't *really* dated. At first I thought he wouldn't have to know. I would just have an abortion and continue to plan my move. Another child would only slow me down. Although I was leaning toward having an abortion, the thought weighed heavy on me.

We didn't see each other as often, but Lucas understood me and gave sound advice from a man's point of view. "D, you don't need another baby. Damn, Brittany is not even a year old. You need to get it together," he reprimanded me, "Go to college or something and get a degree. You're smart, don't get sucked into this ghetto life, you're better than this!" Before he walked out the door he reached into his pant pocket, pulled out a wad of cash and shoved it into my hand. "Sis, you really need to get rid of that baby." He was advising me to have an abortion. Lucas had solved many of his own problems like this, so in his mind, it was better to take care of this *little* problem now. I looked at him and nodded, but when he left, it wasn't settled in my spirit. I couldn't bring myself to do it. I called Lucas a few days later to give him the news.

"You can come by and get the money, I'm going to keep my baby." He didn't dispute my decision and I didn't expect him to, he insisted that I keep the money. "I want you to use it to buy something for the baby," he said. That's how he was. I laughed at his comment. "Okay, bro. I love you!" He'd support me no matter what I decided because he really wanted the best for me. "I love you, too," he responded.

Things had already been rough, and with two children they would more than likely get worse before they got better. But, the thought of having an abortion made me extremely sad, and I couldn't do it. I was going to have my baby and I'd love that baby as much as I loved Brittany.

I told Santiago about the pregnancy and that I'd considered having an abortion, he was angry and begged me not to do it. "Man, don't kill my baby," he said. Shockingly, he was happy that I was pregnant. "I don't want to raise kids by myself!" I snapped back. "You don't have to, I'll help you," he said. I respected him for that, but his happiness didn't make me feel better about having another child at twenty years old. Santiago had proven from the beginning that he was much more of a man than Napoleon, but I continued to plan my move and nothing was going to stop me. My children would be safe, just as Mama had prayed.

Santiago tried to talk me into staying until the day I left. He wanted us to try to work it out and be a couple. "Just stay here and I will help you take care of the kids. You don't have to move." But I knew in my heart that I had to move. My time here was up and my destiny had to be fulfilled.

Chapter 25

Blessed Assurance

Mama cried most of the way to the Greyhound bus station. I sat on the passenger side perfectly content, and every now and then I'd look in the back seat at my daughter. It was amazing how much she had grown in such a short time. Her braids hung past her shoulders and were adorned with white beads. My baby girl's giggle assured me that she couldn't conceive the transition that we were about to make. I left Ford Heights with a duffel bag and two thirty gallon sized garbage bags.

As we pulled into the bus depot my heart dropped. This was it. Mama opened the car door and walked around to the back of the car to grab Brittany out of her car seat. Before she could unbuckle the seat, Brittany noticed the buses parked neatly in the garage and screamed "I wanna get on the bus." I grabbed her tiny hand and placed her on my hip and kissed her cheek.

Mama grabbed both the garbage bags as Brittany tugged at the duffel bag that I was carrying. "It's too heavy for you," I said. She continued to tug at the bag until I let it go. I had to let her feel the weight of the bag. She struggled to drag it across the floor and finally, she let go. "See I told you," I said with a hearty laugh. I wanted her to know that "fat meat was greasy". The old folks used that saying when they'd constantly given us warnings and we had not headed them. It was like saying, "I told you so," but, without the condemnation. I wanted to teach my children right from wrong early and I would use every opportunity.

People had already begun to board the bus. "De'Vonna, you better get going," mama said. She still had tears in her eyes. "Look, you don't have to be out there living from pillar to post, if things don't work out you always have a home." I heard mama, but something in me knew I'd never move back to Ford Heights. I hugged her as tight as I could. Brittany was content with my mother and didn't cry when I kissed her and made my way to the bus.

My baby didn't understand the journey I was about to take and how it would affect her life as much as it would mine. I waved goodbye to my baby girl from the bus window. I would see her soon, mama was going to drive her to Minnesota after I found a job and settled into an apartment.

I sat on the bus and observed the snow and the trees as we passed through Madison, Wisconsin. I'd never been this far north and couldn't believe I was actually relocating and moving away from my family. I would miss each of my siblings; we'd never been separated from each other.

I would be leaving behind the secrets, and finally I'd be deserting a relationship that had caused me grief for many years. I was leaving it all behind and I felt my spirit being released from my past. Moving from my birthplace hadn't been a small feat, but I knew it would all work out. From the moment I'd decided to move to Minnesota I had peace in my soul, peace that surpassed all of my understanding, and now my faith was unshakeable. It was amazing how clearly one could think when everything was quiet around them.

I was so accustomed to there always being *something* going on, that it was almost strange to be still. And then, I wondered what it must have felt like for the slaves passing through the Underground Railroad junction, Ford Heights. They too, had been physically and mentally enslaved, so when they realized they were almost free and could no longer hear the barking dogs or men chasing them with guns -- it had to have felt like this. Finally I could taste my freedom and I knew the chains had been broken.

There were all kinds of people on the bus – college students, older men, older women, young adults, and people that looked homeless and destitute. Some looked just like me – young mothers, pregnant and in search of a new life. I wondered what their stories were. Maybe they had heard about the good living in Minnesota too. I smiled.

The bus ride had been long and my body was tired. I couldn't wait to get to Fran's apartment so I could take a nap, relax, and start planning for the next phase of my life. I had premonitions that life would be grand in Minnesota, I'd go to college and get a degree and I'd be an example to my children.

When we pulled into the Minneapolis bus depot I waited for everyone to get off the bus. My belly was big, and I didn't want to be bombarded with all the people exiting. When I finally wobbled off the bus I heard a familiar voice scream my name. It was Fran. I hadn't seen her since she moved to Minnesota several months earlier.

"De'Vonna, De'Vonna!" she yelled to me. She hugged me tight and grabbed one of the garbage bags. "Hey, big belly, I'm so happy to see you! Let's go home and feed you and that baby." She was still her usual loud bubbly self. We arrived at her apartment, got settled, and spent hours talking and getting caught up on life. I looked around her apartment for her son and didn't see him. "Where's Lester?" I asked. "He's sleeping," she said. Her son was almost two years old.

Fran and I had gotten up early the following Monday to go to the welfare office. She said she'd show me later where we could sell some of our food stamps to get extra cash. She had advised me that the benefits in Minnesota were a little more than in Illinois.

"You'll get four hundred thirty-seven dollars in cash benefits, and when you have the other baby you'll get five hundred thirty-two dollars in cash." She was so excited. I only wanted to get on my feet and prepare to find a job. I would not be raising my children on welfare. I couldn't imagine living the rest of my life on five hundred thirty-two dollars per month. I figured if I made minimum wage at six dollars and fifty cents an hour I could bring home over one thousand dollars per month and I wouldn't have to worry about state mandates, forms, or dealing with case workers who only considered me another statistic that would age out on welfare. As far as I was concerned, state benefits would be what they were meant to be, a stepping stone. For now I was grateful to find out that I'd get welfare, which included cash and food stamp benefits. I was told that I would receive my food stamps immediately, but wouldn't receive cash benefits for seven to ten days. How would I survive without any cash between now and the next ten days? 'God would make a way.' Besides, I had planned to go job hunting that week anyway.

Fran had given me instructions on how to take the bus back to her house from the welfare office. After being inside the welfare office and filling out what felt like hundreds of forms I collected my food stamps. I walked across the street to the bus, just as Fran had instructed. As I sat on the corner waiting for the bus to come, I was approached by an innocent-looking lady in her early thirties. "Hey, lil mama, you wanna sell some food stamps? I can give you fifty dollars for a sixty-five dollar book of stamps," she said. I thought about her proposition for a few minutes and decided that I really needed cash. Besides, I knew people back home who traded food stamps when they needed extra cash. It wasn't as if I was buying drugs, the extra cash would only make getting through the month much easier.

"Sure, I'll sell you some stamps," I said. Fran and I talked about selling food stamps, so I'd be a step ahead of her. "My mom works in the building across the street. I'll just run inside and go get the cash. Give me the stamps?" I reached down into my purse and opened the envelope containing my food stamps.

I flipped through the food stamp coupons and found a sixty-five dollar book and placed it in her hand. I watched as she entered the building and I waited patiently for her to return. After about twenty minutes she hadn't come out of the building and I started to get nervous. I stood up from the bench and walked towards the building, hoping I'd see her as she walked out, but I didn't. I walked inside the building and stopped at the front desk to ask if anyone had seen her. No one had seen her nor did they know who she was. "Is there another way out of the building?" I asked. Without speaking the receptionist pointed to the door behind her. My heart sank. I couldn't believe I'd been that gullible and allowed someone to take advantage of me. I played out the scene of what I would do to her if I saw her.

I walked out the back door and down the block hoping to see her, but quickly concluded that she was gone. She had probably sold the food stamps by then and was somewhere getting high. Now I'd have to find a job sooner than I expected. There was no way I would make it through the month.

As I got closer to my due date, I realized that I really needed to find an apartment before my baby was born. I applied for an apartment across the hall from Fran and got approved. Initially, I didn't know how I could afford it. My welfare benefits would be five hundred thirty-two dollars per month and my rent would be four hundred seventy-five dollars. There was no way I could survive without employment.

I moved into my own apartment and found a part-time job at White Castle. For the first time in my life I was living a stress-free life. My apartment was very small, but I knew it would be comfortable and just right for my children and me. I was proud to finally realize what responsibility meant, but mama had taught us to be independent to a fault and when I needed something, I had too much pride to ask. Now I was a long way from home and I'd have to learn to do just that. All of my furniture had been donated by an organization that helped single parents get on their feet. I didn't care that my sofa was brown and green, I had something to sit on and I was happy to finally have something to call my own.

The organization had given me a queen-sized bed and a crib. They had also donated dishes, pots and pans and other household necessities, things that I had taken for granted when I lived with mama.

As promised, when I moved into my apartment, mama took time off work to drive Brittany to Minnesota. I couldn't believe how much she'd grown in so little time. "Mama, when is our baby coming?" she asked. I laughed and said, "Soon, I hope, really soon." She would be eighteen months old when the baby was born. She made me so happy, and I would be even happier when the other baby was born.

One would have assumed that my situation was dire, but I was happier than I had ever been! I could walk outside and not hear gun shots and walk my daughter to the park and play outside with her. The streets weren't filled with litter, everything was clean! Drug sales may have been happening around us, but not in broad daylight or out in the open, as it had been in Ford Heights.

Mama loved my apartment, and she was proud of how well I'd done in such a short period of time. She hadn't stayed as long as I wanted her to because she had to get back to work. After I moved to Minnesota, mama and I talked and wrote a lot. We wrote each other letters even on the days that we talked on the phone, so I always knew what was going on in Ford Heights. It made being away from home so much easier. I hadn't realized how resilient my mother was or that her letters had inspired me from many miles away. Mama never thought I was weak or that I couldn't make it, she believed in me when I didn't believe in myself. My mother was so encouraging and whenever I felt down, I'd run to grab one of the letters she'd written me.

January 27, 1994

Dear Pooh,

How are you and the children doing. Fine I hope. All is well. Sometimes I need to talk to you, but being I don't have a phone, and people are so funny about their phone. I just use other peoples phone when I have to. "oh yea". I started school last week, and this is my second week, even on Saturdays. I was so excited, so determined to reach my goal and no one is gonna stop me now. I feel like I belong now. You know what I mean (a part of society) Last week my car wouldn't start, believe it or not, I caught a ride in the tow truck with him. The next day, I walked up to Brenda's and she took me. Saturday I caught the bus at 7:30 A.M. to the bus terminal, no bus runs to Prairie State on Saturday. Caught a cab to school (paid $3.50) caught a cab back to bus terminal $3.50 more. Waited 1/2 hour the bus to bring me home. Now I know what determination really mean now. I just really found out last week. So lets keep on doing and try to reach your goal. and so will I. maybe some day we will be side by side in some kind of business or employment together.

Love ya!
Mom.

My mother was a trooper and I noticed that though I'd moved over five hundred miles away to change my life, my mother was making her own transformations. After she left, I missed her so much.

I put Brittany in her stroller and walked to Kmart. On the way back, the walk seemed longer. The baby had dropped deeper into my abdomen and my lower back ached. I would be giving birth in less than a month. I looked up when I thought someone was speaking to me. When I glanced over towards the house, I saw her. She was a harmless looking lady a few years older than me. Her daughter was hanging onto her leg. She'd yelled from her front porch, "Girl, that belly of yours is huge; you need help with them bags?" After the food stamp incident, I wasn't taking any chances. I looked at the stranger cautiously, but after using discernment I concluded that she wasn't a con artist, "Sure, why not?" I really needed help. "Whuuu yo' name?" Brittany asked. "My name is Janice. I live right next door. "I'm De'Vonna. I just moved here a few months ago."

After a lengthy conversation we realized that she'd lived in Ford Heights for much of her life and we knew many of the same people. I was shocked that we didn't know each other, but understood that the only reason we didn't was because of our age difference. Janice had lived in Minnesota for over a year, so she had a gauge on how things worked. We had gotten very close over a short period of time, and it was obvious that this friendship was not a fly-by-night connection; this girl would be in my life for years to come. Brittany and I spent a lot of time at Janice's house and she visited us often.

When I received a phone call from my brother Bryce, I figured Mama must have really rubbed it in after her visit. Minnesota was a great place to live and to raise children, and she was now encouraging her sons to make the move to better their lives. Both of my older brothers each had a child and though they were young, they had shown that they would be good fathers.

I knew mama was proud of how I had turned my life around, but I wondered what she could have said that would make my brother now want to relocate.

"There is no way you are leaving Ford Heights," I teased him. "You'll see," he said. My older brother was the patriarch of our family. He'd protected us when mama wasn't home or when she was working, just as I had been the matriarch in her absence. Children in single family homes often bear the responsibility of the absent parent and we had both been forced into roles that we weren't ready for. The experience of being in charge had given us the ambition to make choices that would affect our lives and our families. He said he'd already made plans to come to Minnesota the following month. I secretly wished it was sooner. I was lonely and missed my family. When my brother's fiancée, Toni called to confirm that they were indeed moving to Minnesota, I was ecstatic. They had dated all through high school and she'd been a part of our family for so long that we were more like sisters than in-laws. With my due date approaching I was happy that they were considering moving to Minnesota. It meant that I wouldn't have to give birth alone, without family. Their daughter was the same age as Brittany, and now she'd have a playmate. This was great news. The countdown was on and I could hardly focus. Bryce had wasted no time and he was in Minnesota three weeks later. He found a job at a recycling company a week after their relocation and they moved into my apartment building.

Fran had become standoffish towards me and stopped answering my phone calls. That really bothered me, and I hadn't figured out what was going on until Paula called me asking what had happened. "Girl, what is going on with you and Fran?" I was a bit taken back because I wasn't aware that there was any friction.

Fran thought "I was arrogant and I had changed." I was very sad to hear that, and I wished Fran would have expressed her feelings to me. I agreed with part of her assessment. I had *changed*. I was a mother, and I was pregnant with my second child. Most definitely, I'd changed. There was no way I could continue to live the way I did when I was single and in my teens. I had children to protect and to be an example for, but I didn't think I was better than she was. I just wished we could   both   be   better   together.

Chapter 26

Smile, Baby, Smile

"Push now, you have got to push, or it's going to take you all day to have this baby," the nurse said. "I can't, it hurts," I cried and grunted without screaming. I was determined not to scream, I could do this without screaming. I was in labor, but I could only focus on how cold the room was. The sheet that fell between my hips and my knees was very thin, and the County's mission to make welfare moms feel uncomfortable while giving birth as single parents had been achieved. The nurses hadn't been very cordial or patient with me. I assumed it was because the State of Minnesota was paying for the birth of my second child and I didn't have the luxury of having a husband's insurance to cover the cost. I was demeaned, and wondered what the childbirth experience was like for women who had private insurance. I imagined them lying on Serta mattresses with one thousand thread count sheets, drinking champagne and eating caviar. Of course they were joined by their husbands and grandparents from both sides of their families.

I lay in the hospital bed pushing out my second child and except for my brother's fiancée Toni, I was alone. No husband, no grandparents, just Toni and I. Here I was sitting in the cold welfare ward in a room being looked down on. 'You wait, you just wait, Ms. Nurse Lady,' I thought. 'One day I'm going to give birth, and I will have top notch insurance, and you will look upon me with respect.' I imagined telling the nurses as a contraction hit me. I wasn't going to allow them to see weakness in this poor, welfare mom. "ARRGGGGHHH!" I grunted. I was not going to shed a tear. "It will be okay," Toni repeatedly said. She sat in the chair next to the bed and coached me as best as she could. My brother had driven back to Chicago that weekend and Mama had asked Toni if she would at least stay until I gave birth. They had planned their trip back to Chicago several weeks earlier, but she had been kind enough to postpone her trip until I had the baby. I'd been having contractions all weekend. The pain was almost unbearable, but I'd told myself I could do this without screaming. I didn't want to cry, I just wanted to give birth to this baby and get it over with. I could be strong, I could keep pushing and eventually the baby would be here.

"Come on, one final push, Ms. Bentley, and your baby is here. I can already see the head." The nurse nonchalantly cheered me on. I clamped my hands down on the iron posts on both sides of the bed and let out a grunt that followed with a sigh of relief, and I knew my baby had entered the world. I was exhausted.

"It's a girl," the nurse said as she placed the suction into my infant's nostrils to suck out mucus and fluids. I smiled and anticipated the moment she would be brought to me.

"Is she okay? Is she healthy?" I asked.

"Yeah, she's fine," the nurse responded dryly.

I dropped my head on the pillow and tears ran down the side of my face. I had considered aborting this beautiful baby and there she was, perfect.

I thanked God for allowing me to give birth to a healthy baby. I was so happy, and when I looked over at Toni, she was crying too. She had witnessed the birth of my beautiful baby girl. After the formalities, the nurse brought my baby over to me and laid her on my chest. I placed my hands on her back and kissed her cheek. She was the most beautiful thing I'd ever seen. I know I'd hoped for a boy, but the joy that this little girl brought me was unlike anything I'd ever felt before.

Toni and I agreed that she resembled a Native American. She had a full head of black hair, and once again I was in love. I named her Alexis, my beautiful Alexis.

I was suddenly frightened by the responsibility that was now before me. 'How am I going to take care of two children on my own?' I thought. When I looked down at my baby girl, she smiled. 'I didn't realize babies smiled so soon,' but my baby girl had looked deep into my eyes and smiled. I knew this was no coincidence. I was relieved, and all traces of fear were gone. I took it as a sign that everything would be okay because I had just been reassured by the angel God entrusted me with.

Alexis, 2 months old

Chapter 27

Dreams, Big Dreams

I worked at White Castle until Alexis was born, but the pay was not enough to make ends meet, I needed more money. Six weeks after Alexis was born, Toni and I had gone to a temporary agency to apply for jobs. We'd heard that they were hiring on the spot for janitors working third shift. We were both hired on the spot and started working that same evening. My brother had agreed to babysit my daughters. It wasn't a glamorous job, but the pay was decent and it was full time. Our duties were to dump the trash in the offices, vacuum, and clean the bathrooms. My favorite duty was to dump the trash bins in the offices. I had my reasons.

I'd walk through each cubicle, pick up the trash, and glance over at the pictures on the desks. Some of the photos featured families with children, a husband and wife with no children, and some cubicles had no pictures. The cubicles with pictures told a story, and most of them seemed to have happy endings.

That's what I had imagined for my life, a happy ending. One day I'd have a cubicle, and I'd make sure to put up pictures of my girls and me. I imagined Alexis' big smile and laughed to myself. She was such a happy baby. Her personality was large for a new born, I missed her. I imagined that one of the cubicles were mine. I looked at the picture and placed myself in their homes and daydreamed of one day having a big house with a white picket fence.

My brother had taken us to work and picked us up for several weeks in the beginning until his car broke down. The supervisor offered us a ride to and from work and suggested we only give him money for gas. This arrangement worked for a few weeks until he started making advances toward me. I didn't want to jeopardize our ride to work, so I brushed it off whenever he rubbed up against me or touched me inappropriately. I really needed my job and couldn't afford to be out of work. Toni assured me that their car would be fixed in a week or so, I just had to hold on until then. "Okay, but that car better get fixed soon because I can't take much more of this," I told her.

And then, one evening at the end of our shift, the supervisor smacked me on my butt, and I'd had it with his sexual harassment. I waited for him to get in the car and said, "I'm not interested in you, I will give you money for gas and that's it. You're getting nothing else from me! Keep your nasty hands off me you disrespectful pervert!" This man had worn on my patience, making passes at me every night, and touching my butt at every opportunity after I'd asked him repeatedly not to.

"You *heffas* can find your own ride to work then," he said. I looked at him with venom in my eyes. "I would rather walk to work than sleep with you!" Before I could complete my next thought he pulled over to the curb. We knew what that meant and we politely got out of his car. Toni looked back at the car as it skid off and left us standing on the curb. Our temporary assignment had been located in a highly populated business area, but there were no buses running in the area late at night. It was after midnight.

"We have each other, right," I told Toni. We both laughed, and she reminded me that I could have at least waited until we got home to tell him off.

We walked to the nearest gas station and called a cab.

The following morning I went to see my caseworker at the Employment Action Center; I was mandated to check in with her monthly. During our discussion, I expressed to her that I needed a skill, one that would sustain me and provide enough income to live off.

I was interested in becoming a hair stylist, at least until my kids were older, and then I'd pursue traditional college courses. The jobs that I had been getting weren't paying me the kind of money I needed to provide a stable life for my children. She suggested I enroll in a business program. "Your aptitude tests all prove that this is a perfect fit for you, and since you have many clerical skills I have to recommend you to a business college," she said. "You could very easily start out as a secretary and work your way up to an administrative assistant. I'm sorry, but the State will not allow you to be on welfare and pursue a career in cosmetology. It's not the kind of profession that we believe will sustain you long term," the case worker said. I had taken three buses just to have her tell me what my career choice should be.

It was my life, and I should be able to do whatever kind of work I wanted to do. I had no say in what my career would be and I never would as long as I was on welfare. I was angry. Did they even consider the chances of me actually staying in a job that I didn't like long term? I'd been optimistic about the county's initiative to fund the educational goals of clients, but today my dreams had been shattered. It was the middle of the month; I had no car, no money, and no future plan that made sense. Not only was I out of a job, but I'd lost my enthusiasm for the one thing that I loved, because I'd been told that if I went to school for cosmetology I'd lose my welfare benefits. There was no way I could afford to attend school without any financial support. When I returned to my apartment, I didn't pick the girls up right away; I wanted time to myself, to sort things out in my head. I didn't want them to see me cry, and that day I needed to shed tears. I could not take care of two children on my own; this load was too hard, too much for me to bear. I decided that I would call mama later to ask her if she'd be willing to take the girls for a few months until I got things in order.

I wanted to find a stable job, maybe two jobs, save some money and try to buy another car. In my mind, today's news was major and it was a set back. I cried for hours and fell asleep in the middle of the day.

Chapter 28

The Evidence of Things Unseen

When I woke up from my nap I walked to Kmart to grab a few things before I picked the girls up. I had twenty dollars to my name and would not get my final check from the temporary agency for another week. Alexis needed diapers. I walked to the back of the store and looked at the different brands and compared prices. The Pampers brand was thirteen dollars and ninety-nine cents, and the generic brand was six dollars and ninety-nine cents. If I got the generic brand I'd have thirteen dollars left until next week, but if I got the Pampers brand I'd have only six dollars left over. My welfare check wouldn't come for another thirteen days. But, I couldn't allow my baby to wear the cheap generic diapers because they had given Brittany a painful diaper rash that not even the home remedies could heal. I made the sacrifice and chose the Pampers.

As I was on my way out of the store, I noticed all the cute little girl clothes and began to browse. I wished I could afford to buy the girls something new.

I couldn't afford anything. I was poor and that was the reality. I stood in the aisle at Kmart contemplating if I should take the clothes or not and had decided that my babies deserved it. I wouldn't make a habit of it, and it would be just this one time. I mean, I'd shoplifted before for dumb reasons, but this time I was doing it for a good reason. I stuffed the outfits in my large bag and walked out of the store. I wanted the best for my girls. Suddenly, I noticed that two men had followed me out of the store. They were loss prevention agents, "Miss, we need you to come back into the store with us." I wanted to run, but I knew I was guilty and what I had done was wrong. I didn't resist. I was immediately guilt ridden, 'why would I do something so stupid?' I hadn't thought of my daughters. I was led to the back of the store to provide the agents with my identifying information while we waited for the police to show up. I was then escorted down the store's main aisle in handcuffs and taken downtown to the county jail. I'd never spent a night away from my daughters! I hadn't thought of the repercussions of what I'd done or how it would affect my children.

I had no idea how long I'd be there and I'd never spent a night in jail before. I was booked, shown to my cell, and given one thin sheet that didn't look clean. The cell was cold and dark. There was a commode in the cell and no privacy. If you had to relieve yourself everyone could see you. In each of the cells the women looked as if they were accustomed to being there. They were drug addicts, prostitutes, and alcoholics, and seemed to know the system very well. They answered all of my questions about lockup.

"Oh yeah, this is your first offense? Girl, you'll be out of here on Monday. If today was Thursday, you would be out tomorrow," they told me. It was just my luck, I'd gone to jail on a Friday and I'd be there until Monday. I shared a cell with a woman who had been picked up for prostitution. She said the County was "messing with her money."

"Quiet down in here! Lights out!" the guard yelled as the lights were all shut off. All I could think about was how stupid I'd been. My brother was so angry with me when I called to explain my whereabouts. "Why in hell didn't you tell me you needed money? You know I would have helped you with the girls whenever you needed help. This is unnecessary."

He was right; I hadn't asked anyone for help with the girls. Once again, he was forced into the "father role," and I knew he'd bail me out on Monday. I thought about all the bad choices I'd made in my life. None of them compared to what I'd done today, there was no real excuse for this. I had come to Minnesota to change my life. I had changed my life and I was doing so well, but in a matter of minutes I'd made a dumb mistake, all for nothing!

For two nights I sat in the cell staring at the bible that lay next to the bed. At first I'd looked at it and I had gotten angry. 'God hadn't been there for me. 'Where was He when I was being abused? Being raped? Huh? Where was He? He was up there, *sitting high and looking low.* I'd heard my grandparents say it on so many occasions,"God sits high and He looks low." I couldn't understand how He had so much control, but not enough control to prevent me from going through the things I'd gone through. Why would I, want to pick up a bible? Regardless of the strong feelings I had, I was still drawn to it, and eventually I reluctantly picked it up, and it fell open to Nehemiah, chapter 2: 17-18

Then I said to them, "You see the trouble we are in: Jerusalem lies in ruins, and its gates have been burned with fire. Come, let us rebuild the wall of Jerusalem, and we will no longer be in disgrace." I also told them about the gracious hand of my God on me and what the king had said to me. They replied, "Let us start rebuilding." So they began this good work.

At that very moment it had become clear to me that I needed to start rebuilding. I needed to completely change my mindset. I was no longer in the projects; therefore, I needed to learn different survival techniques. I could not put new wine in old wineskins! From that day forward I would depend on God to show me how to survive. He'd be the one to start making all the decisions. After I read that passage of scripture I began to believe that God loved me, and no matter what had happened to me. It was time for me to move from a place of depression and oppression to victorious living. My thoughts had not completely lined up with where God was trying to take me. In Nehemiah, the scripture said "let us start rebuilding," and I knew what it meant, I needed to start allowing God to rebuild my life from the very root.

I snapped out of it when the guard called my name.

"De'Vonna Bentley, you're out of here." I had been waiting to hear those words for two days. In Illinois, if you got caught shoplifting you would be out within an hour as long as your fingerprints came back clean. I couldn't believe I had been booked, fingerprinted, and charged with a misdemeanor for a first offense. When the guard called my name I was calm, but deep inside I was secretly jumping for joy. There were still people waiting to get out of this place, yet I was being released. 'Thank you, Jesus!' I missed my daughters terribly. I promised God that I would never shoplift again or touch anything that didn't belong to me. I'd never commit another crime.

The guard handed me a yellow slip which turned out to be a mandate to attend a theft deterrent program. 'What? They were actually forcing me to attend a program for people that had real issues.' I didn't have issues; I had just made a mistake. One mistake! The classes were mandated with the understanding that all charges would be dropped once the classes were finished. That was the best part of the deal because I didn't need the class otherwise and I definitely didn't want a criminal record.

Chapter 29

Unrealized Capacity

"My name is De'Vonna, and I am a shoplifter."

There were fifteen other people in the classroom, and they had easily said it. I was not a shoplifter, and I didn't have a problem with shoplifting, but I could not move on unless I said it. I sat in the roundtable session with my arms folded.

"I can do whatever else you want me to do, Ms. Nedlemier, but I am not a shoplifter," I jokingly said. Finally, I'd had enough and decided this class would only last as long as it was supposed to. "Okay, okay I'm a shoplifter," I said with attitude. That didn't make her happy. "That's not the tone you need to be using, Ms. Bentley," she said. I finally gave the class what they wanted. "I am a shoplifter," I had said it. The theft deterrent class examined several reasons for shoplifting, including poverty, abuse, or drugs, and had lasted a full week.

I had gotten used to having something positive to do everyday. I'd actually found out a lot about myself that week. We were given career assessments, and I found out that I really liked working with people.

Ms. Nedlemier had requested that I "hang tight" after everyone else left the classroom at the end of our final session. We all said our goodbyes and some of us even hugged. The week had been intense. There were writings, take-home assignments, testimonials, and other to-dos that were required. I had no idea why she'd asked me to stay after everyone else had left. All I could think of was that I'd miss my bus and another one wouldn't come for twenty minutes. After the last person left the room she sat down at the table facing me.

"De'Vonna, I have enjoyed meeting you this week. I know it was hard for you to join in the first day, but I'm glad you finally came around. I don't know what you have been through in your life or what brought you to this point, but this doesn't have to be the end. I feel like I'd be doing you an injustice if I didn't speak with you personally. You are one of the most articulate people that has ever come through my program.

You have the potential to do whatever you want to do."
I was speechless. I had never heard anyone say those
words to me other than mama. A professional had said
to *me* that I had potential.' Now, I stood there, almost
embarrassed to hear those words.

"Thank you. No one has ever said that to me before. It
means so much," I said. She hugged me, wished me
good luck, and we parted ways. The feeling was
euphoric. That day I realized how much an
encouraging word could change a person's life. A light
went off in my entire being and I knew I would be
okay. I was *supposed* to be in that classroom that week. I
was supposed to get caught shoplifting! God had
predestined it, and my life would never be the same. In
fact, much of everything that had happened in my life
had occurred for a reason and I was finally beginning
to accept that. I began to make choices about my life
that were geared toward my future – a future that was
bright and full of the potential to be blessed, and to be
happy. I had the potential to be a woman who could be
loved and respected. I deserved those things, and my
children deserved those things. From that day forward
my life changed dramatically. After the theft deterrent
class I went through a transformation.

My brother Eric called to check on me, he'd always been my biggest supporter and he didn't know how much his encouragement added to the changes that were already taking place in my life. He was a preacher at heart and didn't know it. He prayed with me first and suggested that I register for college, "you can do it," he said. "You may as well start college now because time will keep moving no matter what you're doing."

I didn't waste any time, I immediately registered and started attending classes at the community college. I continued to work long-term assignments through several temporary employment agencies.

It seemed I always had work and a paycheck with no lack or lag and things were looking up for me. The girls were both in preschool and day care. I'd found a church to attend, bought a used car, and moved to a more affordable apartment through a transitional program for single parents. I had phased off of welfare, with the exception of child care assistance because child care was simply unaffordable for a single parent with two children.

Bryce had been working at a chemical plant, and he referred me for an Accounting Clerk position that was available. I'd worked through temporary agencies as a receptionist, clerical staff, and administrative assistant, but I didn't have an accounting background. Regardless, God was making a way for me; I was hired on the spot after negotiating my yearly salary of $35K! I never imagined making that kind of money. It was 1995 and I was more blessed than I had ever been.

Chapter 30

Beauty for Ashes

It was dark and I could barely see my hands in front of my face. I held on tight, nervously gripping the steering wheel, knowing that if I let it go I wouldn't make it to my destination. 'Where was my destination?' I didn't know, all I knew was that I had to keep driving. My speed accelerated as I drove for miles trying to make sense of the scenery. I slowed down as I made out a figure standing on the side of the road. The shadow began to take shape as I closed in on him. There he stood next to a large dead tree that continued to push dead roots above ground and onto the land. The buildings began to take shape and I knew I'd seen them before. The project unit where I'd been born and raised stood there with windows shattered and the doors boarded up with pieces of wood. I still didn't understand why I was there, 915 East 15th Street; where we'd had so many struggles, and many memories, some good and some bad.

I had to keep driving. As I drove for several miles, I turned and looked on the side of the road.

The figure I'd seen up the road was now clear and I stopped the car. He had been awaiting my arrival, waiting to taunt me and to revive feelings that I had secretly buried. He stood on the corner laughing with a possessed look in his eyes. It was the uncle that had molested me when I was eleven years old. Distraught and confused, I pulled off and continued to drive. My hands were shaking as I held on to the steering wheel.

As I drove further up the road, I shrieked when I saw my daughter standing on the corner crying! My eyes connected with hers and she reached out for me -- but the car would not stop nor would it slow down. I pumped the brakes harder pressing my feet into the pedal with all my strength, screaming "stop, stop, stop!" I screamed louder, but the car continued to accelerate until I could no longer see her. I wept profusely. She was no longer visible. I felt my breath leaving my body.

The nightmare jolted me out of my sleep and I hurried into my daughters' room to make sure they were both okay. I was relieved that they were still sound asleep.

I got down on my knees between their twin beds and I wept. I prayed for God to keep them safe and I prayed for Him to heal me from the hurt and the shame. While my daughters were sound asleep in their beds I was on my knees praying for them and praying for myself. "God, I cannot continue like this. You have to help me. I can't protect my babies twenty-four hours a day, only you can."

Like a zombie I walked back into my bedroom, and I knew what I had to do. I had to finally come to terms with the things that had happened to me and I had to sound the alarm. I could no longer suffer in silence and shame. Everyone in my family needed to know that I had been victimized. I'd start with my mother. I climbed into bed and reached over to grab the phone. I sat up and wrapped the comforter around me for support as I gathered my thoughts.

There was no good way to tell mama all that I had to say, I'd have to just say it - let the words do their own thing. I looked up at the clock. It was three-forty five in the morning. Mama dreaded phone calls that came at odd hours, but I knew she'd answer right away. She needed to know *now*.

I thought I was over it and that I could pretend that those things never happened, but there had always been *triggers*. Gossip from back home triggered feelings of hurt and shame. For years, I thought I was okay because I was prospering. I had a beautiful family, a job, friends, and a home. I had acquired most of everything that I'd only dreamed of when I was a kid growing up in the projects. I had grown spiritually and mentally and had become a mentor and a confidant to many. But, I continued to secretly hate the people that victimized me, and *I wished they would all get what they deserved one day*. When I'd gotten word that my cousin Damien had been charged with rape, it triggered memories. People had made comments about the girl he allegedly raped. "She was a crackhead," they said. But, I believed her, and I wished I could be there to comfort her. I knew what he was capable of, yet I kept quiet and my secret remained hidden. I wished I could have told her that she wasn't alone, and that I was proud of her for reporting him. Even in a broken state she'd had the strength to report him and he had been charged with rape. I believed her when no one else did and I secretly saluted her.

I knew he'd pay for what he had done -- just like my preschool teacher had *paid* for what he had done. He had been killed in a motorcycle accident. After his funeral services, some of the neighborhood people were standing around and going on and on about "what a shame it was that Jim had died in a motorcycle accident." I remembered thinking, 'That's what happens when you molest little kids. God kills you.' And then, when Rashad was sentenced to over forty years in prison, I secretly celebrated the jury's decision.

Though, my life was moving ahead full speed, I had been mentally stuck. I'd never felt worthy of any of the blessings that God had bestowed upon me. I felt dirty, impure, unqualified, and sick. I didn't know how to receive my freedom until now, but freedom had come at a price. I had to accept the things that had happened and be prepared to overcome them. It had been too long and I had to tell my mother, I knew I wouldn't have peace until I did. In truth, I hadn't fully come to terms with the things that had happened and it had brought me to this moment. I dialed my mother's number, the phone rang and she answered.

"Ma, I need to tell you something. This is the hardest thing that I've ever had to do in my entire life. I'm sooo scared right now. So scared, Ma, but I have to say this." I knew Mama was bracing herself, she had no idea what I was about to say, but she knew it was serious.

"Okay baby," she said. My entire body was shaking, but I kept going. It had been a long time coming. "It has kept me hostage for soooo long, Mama. I have blamed you for so many years for what happened to me. I blamed you for not being there and for not protecting me, but *now* I know it wasn't your fault mama." I could hear my mother choke up. "What happened, baby? What happened?" she screamed. Before I could retreat I blurted it out, all of it, the words escaped my lips. All that had happened to me, my mother was finally hearing it, for the first time. All of it, in full detail, and I didn't stop talking until I'd said everything that Mama needed to hear. "It's been eating at me for many years ma, and I'm so sorry that I never told you." I had said it. And, when I did, a weight was lifted and I felt light. I wasn't ashamed now that everything was out in the open, but mama had retreated.

The phone went quiet, and at first I thought my mother had hung up, but I immediately realized that mama was in shock. Her cries were muffled, but I heard her loud and clear. My mother groaned in agony, it was as if someone had shot her in her stomach. Her pain was intense and I felt it five hundred miles away.

"I'm not mad at you mama, you did the best you could." Her pain echoed through the phone. "I forgive you Mama, I do, I forgive you, and I love you." Mama cried. "De'Vonna, I am soooooo sorry, I didn't know, I didn't know." I wished I could be there to hold her as she endured this pain. What had happened to me was out of my mother's control. My mother went through a range of emotions. "I would give my life for you kids and you know that, why didn't you tell me?!!" Mama screamed. She was angry, sad, and guilt ridden. She felt that she had let me down. She called my grandmother that morning to tell her of my confession, but my grandmother was adamant that it did not happen and that I was not telling the truth. This was the same reaction that I feared as a child. I felt sorry for my grandmother and all the other children that would grow up in her home. My heart ached for them.

It didn't matter because I had been healed by the confession of my abuse. I was no longer angry with any of my oppressors, not one of them. I was now free to love, free to forgive, and free to continue to love my children without guilt or shame. I was free to open myself up to real love fully, in a way that I had never experienced it before. I knew that God loved me and I didn't have to fear anything or anyone. I was no longer afraid of what people would say or think because I hadn't done anything wrong.

It was suddenly clear to me why my soul was at stake on the dreadful day of the "exorcism." Many of the girls that had been molested or raped around me were now struggling with mental health issues, drug addictions, and other self defeating behaviors. I'd been renewed by Elder Hutton's prayers. When he prayed for me and anointed my head with oil, I was cleansed by the power of God.

When the strategic attacks were planned against me, the goal was to kill the root of my potential. Before I realized who I was the devil *knew* who I was. He knew that I'd have two beautiful daughters and if he could change my destiny he'd surely change theirs.

He also knew that one day I'd volunteer at juvenile detention centers mentoring girls that had gone through the exact things that I had overcome. These girls needed to hear people say, "You can make it, because I am the living proof."

I realized that what I went through wasn't just about me, but it was so much larger than me. God had begun to show me that His plan for my life was so much more than I could ever imagine. My testimony would extend far beyond my family and Ford Heights, Illinois, and it would be *POWERFUL!* It would heal many.

Abuse of any kind creates "blurred boundaries," which in turn creates a *breading ground* for unhealthy relationships, drug addiction, oppression, and other self-defeating behaviors.

Silence breeds abuse and if we don't expose abuse, we give power to it. And, when we give power to it, we create opportunities for it to happen to *many* others over and over again. No predator deserves that kind of opportunity.

Epilogue

Love's Epiphany

I turned over onto my pillow. I wasn't ready to wake up, but I knew I had to. I was being beckoned by my husband, Robert. He had called my name several times and I still had not responded. When we met, my daughters were eight and nine. He was smart, trustworthy, hardworking, and articulate. He had a brilliant mind and love letters were shared between us until the day we united in holy matrimony. He earned my trust and he'd earned my love. This man had come into my life and loved me unconditionally. He was tall, handsome, and a man of few words. But, when he spoke, people listened. He had integrity, the trust of many, and most of all he loved God. He'd become the father to my children.

"Yes," I answered finally as I turned over to look for him. He didn't respond and I realized I had been dreaming. I laughed, because surely my husband had already left for work, and surely he had already gently kissed my cheek as he did before he left for work every morning.

Being an early riser, he often turned the light on to remind me that I needed to get up too. I'd snuggle my head into the pillow and beg for twenty more minutes before I'd eventually rise. Most mornings he was my alarm clock and I was so accustomed to him waking me up. I laughed, thinking of how often I'd heard him call my name. "De'Vonna, you'd better get up or you're going to be late." When we were dating I loved to hear him call my name, and I'd ask, "What's my name again?" intently waiting to hear the voice that motivated me to do better and to be better. His voice was heavenly. When he'd repeat it, I'd giggle like a teenage girl with a newfound love. That was fourteen years ago!

Thinking back -- I am reminded of how he had seen me through a metamorphosis. I hadn't shared everything with him immediately about the abuse that I'd endured because I'd been deeply ashamed. Each year I'd trusted him more with little pieces of me and I had allowed him in. As I rolled over to get out of bed, I noticed that he'd left a card on the pillow. I shook my head and smiled. I could hear his velvet smooth voice reading to me.

My Dearest De'Vonna,

I am really excited that you are moving forward with your book. I just wanted to encourage you to do it with boldness. Some things that have happened to you are truly unfortunate, and I am sure difficult to talk about, but I think that it is important that you feel empowered to tell your story without any inhibitions. I am proud of you, and I will stand by you whatever the story is. I will not allow you to feel ashamed of anything that has happened to you because none of this was your fault.

God has ordained me to be a covering for you, I can not fail at this; you are so much more to me than just my wife. God blessed me with you and I want to honor him for his gift to me. I think that you are the most beautiful woman in the world and when God created you, it was for me as well as all of those that need to hear your story. I love you, and nothing will ever change that.

Tears streamed, but this time they were tears of joy. And I knew that I was free. Finally. Whole and complete. The journey towards self discovery had been revealed.

The battle had begun when I was five years old and the truth that had once been so shameful and frightening could no longer hold me hostage.

My husband assured me of what God had been saying to me all along. That, no matter what I'd been through or how long I had suffered, that I deserved to be loved and in spite of all my struggles God had the power to heal me. I was free from all that I'd endured, free to love myself and others with no inhibitions. I was finally free to move forward with no guilt, and I was finally free to tell my story, without shame, and without fear.

Robert and De'Vonna Pittman

July 2000

9th Grade
15 Years old

De'Vonna (16) & Paula (18)
Years old

De'Vonna, 1988
(16 years old)

Mama and Ron
1977

The girls and I, 1992

Ron and I

The girls and I, 1994

The girls, 1996

Alexis, Robert, Brittany - 2009

Mama and I, 2002

Robert and I, 2009

Acknowledgements

God ordained this book at my birth. I thank Him for making it possible and for allowing me the time to complete such a delicate project. To my siblings, Bryant, Terry, Latina, Joann, Johnetta, and John...each of you showed me what it meant to share. To my stepfather John (Ron) who showed me what to look for in a man. To the Pittman clan, I love you!

Mama, there are not enough words to express my love for you. Even as a wild child you loved me back to life. When I hear Bet Midler's "Wind beneath my wings," I think of you because you have been just that to me. I love you to the moon!!!! Toon, no matter what, you are there! Laura you already know. You've loved and supported me for years! To my sister-n-laws Tonya and Toya, I love you both. To all of my nieces and nephews, you each make my heart flutter. To Ernest McDonald, Bootsie, *Daddy*, thank you for calling me daughter and for loving me with no bias.

Lori, Laceysa, Melanie, Lamaudia, you have each encouraged me in more ways than you will ever know. Trina, Shana and Lori, you were there at the beginning of my evolution. Whew, what a transformation. My Devastating slims, Freda you've been there ALL my life. Tracey and Sherell I love you forever. Niniea, rest in peace, my love.

LaSonya, the many trips to Caribou kept me sane! Patricia B, Roshonda, Talica, Ebony, and Chandra your support will never be forgotten. Vera and Kendis thanks for always making me laugh. Nesey and Tonia H., your enduring friendship and music cleanses my soul. Latoya & Sernicia, ahhhh…what can I say, I bonded with you two and it was as if we were from the same womb.

Gwen Johnson and Debra Kennedy, my godmothers, I love you both.

Tiffany, my creative consultant where must I begin? You walked side by side with me from the inception of the manuscript and took the journey, cried with me, and laughed with me until the very last word was printed. You are relentless, faithful, diligent, and HONEST. You dove right in and made me dig deeper into the ABYSS…ouch!

Menia Buckner, You are smart, ingenious and articulate. Thank you for the initial edits, the English lessons, and for critiquing *My Pretty* in its infancy.

Tara Stone and Auntie Wanda, thank you for encouraging me from the very beginning.

Nadia and Lorraine, my Jamaican buddies, thanks for loving me into your sisterhood.

Bishop and Mother Daniels, I am so grateful that God led us to Shiloh Missionary Baptist Church. Thank you for your wisdom and for your strong leadership.

TODAH RABA, a huge thank you in Hebrew to my mother-n-law Louella Pittman, a graceful, wise, intelligent, revered, and regal woman. I could spend the rest of my life at your feet and it wouldn't be long enough. To Barb, my Minnesota mama – I know that your prayers have kept me strong.

Sassy, it was meant for evil, but God turned it around for our good. Our children are siblings and we are friends. Sandra, my prayers are with you wherever you are. I look forward to the day I hand deliver your copy of "My Pretty," that is my prayer.

Fran, my beautiful Fran. I haven't forgotten how YOU paved the way for me. God used you to be a vessel to plant the seed for my relocation and transformation. I salute you. I honor you.

Jill Wallace, you knew where I was trying to go with this book. You helped me take it to another level! Thank you for assisting me with the edits and for putting me on the right path. I'm grateful to have had the opportunity to work with you and to have become your friend. Aretta Rie-Johnson, thank you for making me *pretty* in the photos! Regina Wamba at MaeIdesigngraphics! Thank you so much for your patience and skill! You created a book cover that I only imagined in my dreams; you helped me put a bow on it!

In loving memory: Henry and Lucinda Bentley and Bishop Stanley N. Frazier, you showed me how to *really* love God, and to allow him to love me, in spite of what I was going through. Daddy George, may you rest in peace.

My family gives me strength to continue to follow my dreams and intrinsic whims! Some things can not be expressed by mere words - here's my attempt!

A very special thank you to my beautiful daughters, Brittany, my dancer & Alexis, my poet, you two are my heroes. You challenge me to think outside of the box. I'm godly proud of the women that you are becoming and I wouldn't "give nothing for my journey." I thank you both for being BLAZING examples, even to me. This love is still undefined.

To my husband, Mr. Robert Pittman, you have encouraged me from day one. Everything I've accomplished is because you have been by my side. You endured many long nights and lost weekends and dealt with all the paper spread across the kitchen table. Many evenings I bombarded our space to complete this mission and you never complained! More importantly, you encouraged me to write my story and to tell it without fear. Your love and support has sustained me in innumerable ways. Your ferocious love cannot be compared. It feels good to be loved by you, and in return I love you back.

Biography

De'Vonna Bentley-Pittman is committed to providing leadership to end sexual abuse. She earned an Associates degree in Liberal Arts from Minneapolis Community and Technical College and continued her studies at Metropolitan State University where she earned a Bachelors Degree in Human Services with a focus in Community Corrections. She currently serves on the Sexual Violence Center Board of Directors in Minneapolis, Minnesota. She lives with her husband and two daughters. This is her first published work. Excerpts from *My Pretty...and Its Ugly Truth* will be featured in the 2012 Minnesota State Arts Board 8th Annual Art of Recovery exhibit to bring continued awareness to victim's rights.

Crisis Reference Links

1. National Suicide Hotline: 1-800-273-TALK
   Website: http://www.suicidepreventionlifeline.org/
2. National Sexual Assault hotline: 1.800.656.HOPE
   Website: http://www.rainn.org/get-help/national-sexual-assault-hotline

Thank you for reading my memoir. You too, can partner with me in the fight against sexual abuse and sexual violence by speaking out against it in your community and in your family.

Now that you are finished, PLEASE...

Remember to:

- **Rate the book on Amazon.com**
- Tell all of your friends about "My Pretty and Its Ugly Truth".
- Suggest "My Pretty" to your local libraries, schools, organizations, shelters, and book stores.
- Like "My Pretty and Its Ugly Truth" on Facebook
- Follow me on twitter: devonna2
- Request me on Skype: mpait
- Invite me to your book club meeting via skype
- Email me at myprettyanditsuglytruth@aol.com
- If you have a local book club, let's talk
- If you are out of state, let's talk
- For promotional events, contact me at myprettyanditsuglytruth@aol.com

Made in the USA
Lexington, KY
28 February 2012